JESUITS AND JACOBINS

PAUL P. BERNARD

JESUITS AND JACOBINS

Enlightenment
and Enlightened Despotism in Austria

UNIVERSITY OF ILLINOIS PRESS

Urbana · Chicago · London

for E. M.

Preface

SUBJECTS which, in truth, are somewhat lacking in grandeur, such as the one of this little book, present their peculiar pitfalls. The writer either gives in to the temptation of praising his material beyond its merits in order to justify his interest in it, or runs the risk of drowning in a sea of trivia, and he emerges, if at all, as pallid as his material. If I have nevertheless rushed in where generations of angelic scholars have preferred not to tread, it is essentially for two reasons. First, an age as fascinated by the ordinary as ours will surely not blanch at the aspect of literary history from below; the field ought not to be abandoned entirely to the occasional perfunctory Marxist ancestor hunt. And second, the question of "Josephinism" will simply not come to rest. From the myth of Joseph II, the "revolutionary from above," historians have proceeded to the evocation of an equally unsubstantiated, and indeed mysterious, Josephinian *Zeitgeist*, which has in turn been abandoned in favor of, *mirabile dictu*, the admission that there was an actual party of "Josephinians." On closer examination, however, this turns out to be only Prince Kaunitz and two or three trusted assistants, busily engaged in carrying sacks of gunpowder down into the crypt of St. Stephen's Cathedral in Vienna. My purpose is to demonstrate that, such primitive fantasies apart, there were indeed real flesh-and-blood Josephinians, that they are identifiable, and that their opinions form a body that is modest but nevertheless coherent. I am the first to admit that this has been argued before, but I believe this is the first attempt to present the argument in systematic form.

As the reader will soon discover, this tends to be an argumentative piece of work. My opinions obtrude into the text at regular intervals. This is a fault: it is undoubtedly better to let people speak for themselves. If I have not done so, it is not because I feared that, in this case perhaps, their voices might be too weak, but rather because I am engaged in organizing rather diverse materials around a central argument. I hope at least that I have not crossed over from being merely opinionated to becoming actually tendentious. I have also used the terms "liberal" and "radical" throughout in an anachronistic—indeed idiosyncratic—way. As I have explained in the text, I use the first of these labels to describe those who, while willing to work within the confines of a traditional despotism, wished to transform it into the instrument for the introduction of the reforms which they desired largely on theoretical grounds; the second is applied to more adventurous spirits who, although theoretically still content to retain the monarchy, wanted to hem it in with constitutional restrictions to the point where it would have been all but legislated out of existence. I use the terms in question because it strikes me that it is better to commit a conscious anachronism than to resort always to the cumbersome circumlocutions that would otherwise become necessary. It should go almost without saying that Joseph himself cannot be subsumed under either of these categories.

My method has been straightforward. I have read through as much of the literature of the period, both belles lettres and explicitly political material (the social was mostly implicit), as was available to me. Out of this I have culled the materials that impressed me as being most relevant to my subject. This method has resulted in inevitable distortions. Most of the writers whose work I discuss were primarily interested either in the development of strictly literary themes or, more frequently, in ecclesiastical questions. They were not in the first instance, or at least not except for relatively brief periods in their creative spans, social or political commentators, let alone philosophers. Yet I am aware of no very good reason for always preferring a systematic analysis on the grand scale to a merely ad hoc or even casual commentary as material for intellectual history. It may be that in the complex and only imperfectly understood relationship between thought and action one is as germane to the issue at hand as the other. I am also deeply aware that, being neither a literatus nor a political theorist by trade, it is extremely presumptuous on my part to arrogate unto myself the right to speak out on the question of the relationship of literature to political theory. I can only plead that, being tied down by the preconceptions of neither calling, it may just be possible for me to perceive relations that might be apparent only to the outsider. While I can by no means claim to have transformed myself into the *Mann ohne Vorurteil,* I will be content if I have succeeded in challenging with a measure of truth some of the hoarier *obiter dicta* which still infest the study of Josephinism.

LIST OF ABBREVIATIONS

Contents

1 The Austrian Literary Scene

NOT ALL writers of the last quarter of the eighteenth century in Austria were ex-Jesuits. Only a handful, in the event, became Jacobins. Yet the coupling of the two terms is no mere exercise in alliteration. Rather, it touches upon a central if generally overlooked fact of Austrian intellectual life: a by no means negligible number of literati, would-be political commentators, and religious thinkers took the most direct road from a largely uncritical baroque piety to a secularly inspired skepticism. In most cases they did not even stop off at the traditional halfway houses of pietism (rather more of a Protestant phenomenon, in which, in a conscious revolt against the values of late baroque and rococo, German intellectuals, casting desperately about for a German model to follow, finally had to settle: a movement which supplied them both with an approach and a vocabulary),[1] or of Jansenism, although, as we shall see, there were some of the latter persuasion among them. Because Austria did not generally follow the German pattern in which, paradoxically, the spawning ground of secular skepticism was a turning toward religious fundamentalism, it has been assumed that Austria remained mostly untouched by the enlightenment. This was not the case. But it would be foolish to maintain that Austria, by-

---

1. H. M. Wolff, *Die Weltanschauung der deutschen Aufklärung in geistlicher Entwicklung* (2nd ed., Berne and Munich, 1963), p. 62. It is also interesting to reflect on how many German *Aufklärer* were, if not themselves preachers, at least the sons of preachers.

passing the German cultural sphere, received its enlightenment direct and unalloyed from Paris, or even London. This clearly did not happen either. The Austrian literary intelligentsia, as this study intends to show, became aware of Western secular ideas largely through the mediacy of its German counterpart, but interpreted them in the light of its own peculiar and no doubt in many ways insufficient background.

For any of this to take place, there first had to be an intelligentsia in Austria, a fact not generally admitted by all writers on the subject, some of whom habitually portray eighteenth-century Austria as a literary desert. It may well be that by the beginning of the eighteenth century southern Germany had, in the cultural sphere, lost touch with the north; that southern baroque culture tended to value the plastic arts and music more highly than the book; that Spanish Jesuits, important figures at the court of Leopold I, sovereign under Charles VI, allowed themselves to be so dominated by their political animosity for the governments of France and of the Protestant states of Germany that they furthered Hispano-Italian cultural influences to the point that Austria was effectively cut off from what was, for better or worse, the mainstream of Western thought; and that the leading ornament of Austrian letters in this period was the Italian poet Pietro Metastasio, who stylistically may have been a precursor of Austrian classicism but whose works are all but devoid of serious content.[2] Austrian letters were certainly not

2. K. Pfister, *Maria Theresia: Mensch, Staat und Kultur der spätbarocken Welt* (Munich, 1949), p. 240; H. Wagner, "Der Einfluss von Gallikanismus und Jansenismus auf die Kirche und den Staat der Aufklärung in Österreich," *Ö.G.L.*, XI/10 (1967), 521; R. Mühlher, "Die Literatur zur Zeit der Aufklärung in Österreich," *Ö.G.L.*, VIII/6 (1964), 289; J. Nadler, *Literaturgeschichte Österreichs* (2nd ed., Salzburg, 1951), p. 154; H. Pirchegger, J. Mayer, and F. Kaindl, *Geschichte und Kulturleben Österreichs* (3 vols., 5th ed., Vienna and Stuttgart, 1960), II, 265; J. W. Nagl, J. Zeidler, and E. Castle, *Deutsch-Österreichische Literaturgeschichte* (4 vols., Vienna and Leipzig, n.d.), II, 84. To a very limited extent it may be true that the enlightenment in German-speaking countries was an early phase of a German national awakening and thus, necessarily, would have resisted French influences. See G. Wytrzens, "Sur la sémantique de l'Aufklärung," in P. Francastel, ed., *Utopie et institutions au xviiie siècle* (Paris and The Hague, 1963), p. 316.

held in high esteem by contemporaries. On the occasion of a visit to Vienna in 1712 the German philosopher Gottfried Wilhelm Leibnitz elegantly combined a compliment to his aristocratic hosts with a critique of his local rivals by observing that he had found far more in the way of erudition among the gentlemen of Vienna than in the ranks of those who made a profession of letters. And some four decades later the English traveler Thomas Nugent wrote from Vienna that "learning is at present in a state of decline in this country, where there is a greater show of it than reality."[3] Except for their depressing sameness, one could well produce a number of other such judgments. On the basis of literary productions alone, it would be difficult not to sustain them. For instance, in the period 1670–1729 over 300 original novels were published in northern Germany. Not one appeared in Austria. The north was gripped by a rage for literary weeklies, which, while they usually did not maintain themselves for any length of time, appeared everywhere. Austria did not boast a single one until 1762.[4] Nor was the Austrian court inclined to trouble itself considerably to remedy the situation. Johann Christoph Gottsched, a leading figure in the north German enlightenment, was determined to extend his sway over Vienna. To this end, as early as 1728 he sent there a series of increasingly artless panegyrics, praising Vienna as the new Rome. These finally earned him an invitation to visit the imperial court in 1749. But although he was politely received by the Empress Maria Theresa, his offer to found and head an academy of German letters was ignored and Gottsched did not even get what he looked upon as a minimal consolation prize, an appointment as professor at the University of Vienna. So this "Wagner figure in

3. H. Wagner, "Der Höhepunkt des französischen Kultureinflusses in Österreich in der zweiten Hälfte des 18. Jahrhunderts," Ö.G.L., V/10 (1961), 508; E. Menhofer, "Österreich im Reiseführer Thomas Nugents," Bausteine zur Geschichte Österreichs (Vienna, 1966), p. 163.

4. D. Kimpel, Der Roman der Aufklärung (Stuttgart, 1967), p. 22; A. Fischer-Colbrie, Michael Denis: Im schweigenden Tale des Mondes (Graz and Vienna, 1958), p. 6.

Faustian times" was forced to return home empty-handed.[5] It was not until 1761 that the university professor Josef von Riegger, without government help, was able to found the *Deutsche Gesellschaft,* and this organization, not surprisingly, languished for lack of funds. As late as 1775 the great dramatist Gotthold Ephraim Lessing tried to convince the court to put him at the head of this or another officially supported academy, but to no avail.[6]

It has been suggested that the antipathy of the Austrian court for all proposals having to do with the founding or support of semi-autonomous scholarly academies was grounded in a deep-set cultural antagonism: that the north German advocates of a *Gelehrtenrepublik* dreamed of liberties analogous to the corporative freedoms that characterized at least part of the north German political scene. But it seems probable that parsimony rather than principle was at fault. Where an immediate gain could be expected, academies could be founded, even in Vienna, as the creation of the Oriental Academy (1754) for the training of diplomatic and consular officials testifies.[7]

While the foregoing factors may all have played their role, one need not look much further than finances to account for the relative absence of Austrian literature in the first half of the eighteenth century. Even in France the writer who could support himself by his writing was exceptional. In Austria a public which could have bought literary productions in sufficient quantities to make their authors self-sufficient simply did not exist. Patronage was the great thing. And patrons by custom, tradition, and fashion supported the work of musicians, sculptors, and painters rather than that of miserable scribblers. Yet all of these

5. F. Walter, *Wien* (3 vols., Vienna, 1940–44), II, 368; Pfister, *Maria Theresia,* p. 243; Nadler, *Literaturgeschichte,* p. 181.

6. Pfister, *Maria Theresia,* p. 244; Fischer-Colbrie, *Michael Denis,* p. 6; Nadler, *Literaturgeschichte,* p. 181.

7. K. v. Raumer, "Absoluter Staat, Korporative Libertät, Persönliche Freiheit," *H.Z.,* CLXXXIII/1 (1957), 92–93; Pirchegger, Mayer, and Kaindl, *Geschichte und Kulturleben,* II, 325.

limiting factors notwithstanding, there was a considerable reservoir of trained, professional writers in Austria. When, toward the middle of the century, partly as the result of a diplomatic rapprochement with France in the wake of the War of the Austrian Succession, partly as the consequence of a deliberate policy on the part of the crown, there was a literary revival, the men who took pen in hand were neither sheer beginners nor slavish imitators of more advanced cultures. They had been there all along, and even in places where one should expect to look.[8]

The two great repositories of literary talent were nothing more mysterious than the state and the church. At least from the time of Leopold I onward, the Austrian state had maintained a bureaucratic establishment which, because of its imperial as well as its archducal concerns, far outstripped the needs of the average court of the day. Some of these men, perhaps interacting with one another, perhaps merely responding to practical questions confronting them, began to go beyond the routine performance of their tasks. They evolved both a theory and a tradition, which came to be known as Cameralism.[9] Cameralist theory was essentially unalloyed mercantilism, and thus hardly distinguishing for Austria. Moreover, the Cameralists never succeeded in converting the monarch entirely to the system. The only sophisticated theorist among them, Johann Joachim Becker, evolved a sort of populationism that led him to attack the restrictive aspects of the Austrian economy such as guild regulations,

8. For the great increase of French influence in Austria associated with the diplomatic revolution, see Wagner, "Höhepunkt," p. 509. A good statement of the by now traditional thesis that Austria's defeat in the War of the Austrian Succession led to a desperate attempt at reforming the ineffectual military establishment, which in turn necessitated a general overhaul of the whole administrative apparatus, which finally made defenders and propagandists necessary and thus created employment for writers, may be found in H. L. Mikoletzky, *Österreich, das grosse 18. Jahrhundert* (Vienna, 1967), pp. 202–211. See also J. G. Gagliardo, *Enlightened Despotism* (New York, 1967), pp. 86–87, 98.

9. The only full-scale study of the movement is A. W. Small, *The Cameralists* (Chicago and London, 1909), by now badly outdated. The best recent summary may be found in R. A. Kann, *A Study in Austrian Intellectual History* (New York, 1960), pp. 28–31.

but even his system was a mass of contradiction.[10] For instance, he argued for the necessity of creating a ministry responsible for the direction of the whole of the economy, thus possibly being unfaithful to his mercantilistic principles, but as his advice was to some extent followed in practice, it provided future employment for a veritable army of scriveners.

The Cameralist tradition was of a very different order. As developed in Philip Wilhelm von Hörnigk's *Österreich über alles, wenn es nur will* and in the works of Wilhelm von Schröder, it came to stand for the proposition that the highest good was that which accrued to the state, that the welfare of all depended upon that of the state, that there was no higher form of service than state service.[11] Furthermore, the notion of the state is expanded from that of a mere administrative necessity to that of a higher power whose function is to rationalize the direction of economic as well as of political life. Finally, Hörnigk evolves from the assertion that the state must be economically autarkic a higher political meaning, investing the Austrian crown with great power quite independent of its traditional primacy in the Holy Roman Empire.[12] The net result of this was that by mid-century some three generations of writer-bureaucrats had grown up on the teaching that the state must be regarded as primal and were accustomed to look to it not only for their inspiration but also for their sustenance. The poet as bureaucrat, that somewhat unlikely literary hero of Josephinian times, was only one step beyond this.

It must, of course, be mentioned that Becker, Hörnigk, and Schröder were none of them Austrians, the first two being Rhinelanders, the last a Saxon. Moreover, they were all three converts from Protestantism. It might thus be objected that they consequently have no place in a chronicle of what are, after all, Aus-

10. Kann, *Austrian Intellectual History*, pp. 28–29; A. Hoffmann, "Österreichs Wirtschaft im Zeitalter der Aufklärung," *Ö.G.L.*, XII/5 (1968).
11. Small, *The Cameralists*, p. viii.
12. Hoffmann, "Österreichs Wirtschaft," pp. 191, 194, 201.

trian affairs. To exclude them would mean, by extension, to exclude almost half of the important literary figures of the second half of the century, also *Zugereiste,* often in the spiritual as well as the geographic sense. To do so would be wholly unrealistic. These men addressed themselves to Austrian questions, very quickly came to learn the Austrian style in dealing with them, and for the most part their work is indistinguishable from that of the natives of purest blood. To exclude, say, Hörnigk from the ranks of Austrian writers would be the equivalent of maintaining that Metternich was not an Austrian politician.

It has also been argued that the legacy of this bureaucratic literature was pure disaster: that bureaucratic virtues such as the careful weighing of all available evidence before proceeding to action were first elevated to the rank of higher principles and finally had a totally paralyzing effect upon the Austrian literary imagination. Immobilism and static conservatism became life principles. The result was an all-pervasive Austrian mediocrity, severely delimited, absurdly modest in its ambitions, pedantically unimaginative.[13] Whatever the accuracy of these views over the long run may be, in the balance of this study an attempt will be made to demonstrate that for the second half of the eighteenth century they are wildly inaccurate. The bureaucrat-poets of that period, at least, could be and were grossly immodest, sweeping in their ambitions, dynamic and highly imaginative. Nor, as was to be the case with Grillparzer later on, did all of them languish in subsidiary positions, chafing under their inability to change the world and hating the banality of their employment. Some of them, at least, finding jobs in the new combined Bohemian-Austrian *Hofkanzlei,* rose to positions of responsibility and influence.[14] Another center of Cameralist activity was the *Hofkammer.* Because of the fact that it was the agency responsible for producing the extraordinary sums of money that the crown

13. C. Magris, *Der Habsburgische Mythos in der österreichischen Literatur,* trans. M. v. Pasztory (Salzburg, 1966), pp. 15, 26.

14. Mühlher, "Literatur der Aufklärung," p. 292.

periodically required in addition to its regular income, it enjoyed a sort of fool's freedom. From the year 1703 on, when Count Guido von Starhemberg was made its director, it not only maintained a regular correspondence with the Protestant University of Halle, but made a practice of introducing north German Protestants into its service. Thus Vienna was regularly apprised of the latest developments on at least German politico-economic doctrine. Among the most interesting personalities associated with the *Hofkammer* was Christian Schierl von Schierendorff, who in the first quarter of the century produced a spate of pamphlets demanding a greater centralization of the administration at the expense of the Estates, the total liberation of the peasants from their compulsory labor obligations, the adoption of a graduated income tax, and full religious toleration.[15]

To turn to the clerical intellectual tradition, we are faced with not one movement but two—the one orthodox, the other decidedly not. Both, however, produced results which, from the point of view of Rome, were decidedly threatening. That this would turn out to be the case was not for a long time apparent. In the 1730's the Austrian church was thought to be so conservative that even the papal nuncio, Passionei, expressed a desire to see it somewhat liberalized.[16] Had he looked farther than Vienna, he might have tempered this wish. What I have designated the orthodox wing of Austrian progressive clerical thought appeared, shortly after the turn of the century, in a number of loci to the west of Vienna, running from Melk to Innsbruck, and in general was associated with the Benedictine monasteries of the region. In Melk the brothers Pez and in Salzburg the brothers Mezger devoted themselves to critical historical studies in the tradition of Mabillon and the Maurists; and Johann Christoph Barten-

---

15. E. Winter, *Frühaufklärung* (Berlin, 1966), p. 131. For Schierendorff see H. G. Schenk, "Austria," in A. Goodwin, ed., *The European Nobility in the Eighteenth Century* (London, 1963), pp. 102–109; and E. Zöllner, "Bemerkungen zum Problem der Beziehungen zwischen Aufklärung und Josefinismus," *Österreich und Europa* (Graz, Vienna, and Cologne, 1965), p. 209.

16. Winter, *Frühaufklärung*, p. 127.

stein, vice-chancellor of the combined *Hofkanzlei*, dreamed of bringing these learned Benedictines to Vienna to supplant the Jesuits as the intellectual pace-makers of the realm.[17] The secularization of outlook that was characteristic of this school was pushed to its furthest point in the Benedictine house at Kremsmünster, near Steyer. There Placidus Fixelmillner, for many years in charge of the monastery's educational work, while outwardly decrying the excesses of the enlightenment, in fact himself lectured on the advantages it bestowed on mankind, dismissed the Middle Ages as a period of near total darkness, and taught the philosophic system of Christian Wolff.[18] Although in general the Benedictines may be thought to have been exposed largely to Italian influences transmitted through the South Tyrol, Kremsmünster was in addition following the example of Salzburg, then an independent principality ruled by its archbishop but for all practical purposes a part of the Austrian cultural sphere. There Archbishop Leopold Ernst Firmian was not precisely an enlightened despot. Indeed, in 1732 he had made himself notorious by forcibly expelling from his dominions some 17,000 Protestants.[19] Nevertheless, by 1740 a circle modeled on that of Muratori had developed in Salzburg, dedicated to the critical examination of both theological and ecclesiological questions.[20] One of its more prominent members was the Archbishop's nephew, Karl Firmian, who later as Austrian minister to Lombardy was a devoted and enthusiastic supporter of Prince Wenzel Kaunitz' radical ecclesiastical measures, was his whole life an

17. *Ibid.*, pp. 127–128; J. Wodka, "Die Kirche und die Aufklärung," *Ö.G.L.*, X/5 (1966), 228; E. Tomek, *Kirchengeschichte Österreichs* (3 vols., Innsbruck, Vienna, and Munich, 1935–59), III, 130.

18. Wodka, "Kirche und Aufklärung," p. 227; H. Sturmberger, "Studien zur Geschichte der Aufklärung des 18. Jahrhunderts in Kremsmünster," *M.I.Ö.G.*, LIII (1939), 424, 443, 461. The Benedictine publication *Stimmen der Ewigkeit* was saturated with Wolffian philosophy.

19. Tomek's attempt (*Kirchengeschichte*, III, 181–188) to defend the Archbishop by putting the blame on his predecessors whose counter-reformationary zeal had been so lax as to allow the heretics to remain in Salzburg two centuries earlier, while a fair example of his historical objectivity, is not very convincing.

20. Wagner, "Gallikanismus," p. 524.

Anglomane, and for a time contributed generously to the support of the social philosopher and first criminologist, Cesare Beccaria.[21] These unquiet spirits had some influence on events at the University of Salzburg, the conservative nature of whose curriculum entirely reflected the Archbishop's outlook. After a series of unavailing protests, a number of aristocratic students at the university, declaring that they would no longer submit to the old-fashioned regimen that prevailed, departed for various Protestant universities in Germany. The result was, ultimately, a general reform of the curriculum.[22]

The second and decidedly less orthodox intellectual movement within the church was Jansenism. The dominions of the House of Habsburg had from very early times had a penchant for various manifestations of reform Catholicism, and it is at least possible that there is an unbroken line of contacts linking the Czech Hussites of the fifteenth century, the Bohemian Brethren, and the Austrian adherents of the Dutch reformer Cornelius Jansen, and later of his eighteenth-century disciple Johann Nicholas Hontheim (better known as Febronius), auxiliary bishop of Trier.[23] Jansenism-Febronianism was basically a form of Gallicanism, and thus was a movement which insisted on the rights of the national churches vis-à-vis Rome and which stressed the powers of the monarch over the church, a tendency referred to in Austria as *Staatskirchentum*. In addition, Austrian Jansenism

21. A. Wandruszka, *Österreich und Italien* (Vienna, 1958), pp. 61–62.

22. Wodka, "Kirche and Aufklärung," p. 227; Sturmberger, "Geschichte der Aufklärung," p. 433. A similar attempt by young aristocrats to achieve a liberalization of their education took place at the Savoy Academy for Young Nobles in Vienna, but met with little success. The rector, Father Gratianus Marx, complained to the authorities about "das stete naseweise Raisonieren" of his charges and, backed by the full support of Maria Theresa, intimidated them into silence. J. Schwarz, *Geschichte der Savoy'schen Ritter-Akademie in Wien* (Vienna and Leipzig, 1897), p. 110.

23. Wagner, "Gallikanismus," p. 522. For the impact of the earlier movements on Austria, see my "Heresy in Fourteenth Century Austria," *Medievalia et Humanistica*, X (1956); and "Jerome of Prague, Austria and the Hussites," *Church History*, XXVII/1 (1958).

was even more strongly anti-papal and, in particular, anti-Jesuitical.

Jansenism was first introduced in a systematic way into the Habsburg dominions by the eccentric Czech nobleman, Count Franz Anton Sporck. He returned from a visit to France around 1700 determined to put his person and substantial fortune at the service of the reform tendency. On his estate of Kukus in eastern Bohemia he assembled a considerable printing plant which turned out Jansenist books as fast as the originals could be brought from Paris. He let it be known that it was his intention to transform Kukus into an eastern Port Royal. After 1713, when the bull *Unigenitus* condemned 101 propositions in the work of the Jansenist Quesnel, Sporck became a target for the Austrian Jesuits. A landed magnate of considerable fortune was not an enemy to be taken lightly, and at first they proceeded cautiously against him. But, as the Count amused himself by publishing quantities of scurrilous doggerel against the Jesuits, they finally proceeded to obtain the support of the court for judicial proceedings against him. In 1733 Sporck was condemned to pay a fine of 6,000 gold ducats, a judgment to which he submitted. Still, for some thirty years the country had been flooded with Jansenist books and pamphlets, none of which had, as the law required, been submitted for censorship.[24]

A much more unexpected source of Jansenist infection was, of all places, the Jesuit-run institution for the training of German-speaking clergy, the Collegium Germanicum in Rome. Several of the leading figures of Austrian Jansenism, including Archbishops Leopold Ernst Firmian of Passau, Hieronymous Colloredo of Salzburg, Joseph Spaur of Seckau and Brixen, and the auxiliary bishop of Vienna, Simon Stock, not only received their training there, but apparently returned to Austria as con-

---

24. Wagner, "Gallikanismus," p. 523. On Sporck see also E. Winter, *Der Josefinismus* (2nd ed., Berlin, 1962), pp. 17–18; and, in great detail, H. Benedikt, *Franz Anton von Sporck* (Vienna, 1923).

firmed Jansenists.[25] At any rate, by the second half of the century the adherents of Jansenism occupied important positions in the Austrian hierarchy, and now their influence came to be felt at court. The archbishop of Vienna, Cardinal Johann Joseph Trautson, although himself no Jansenist, in 1752 issued a pastoral letter inveighing against various superstitions, including the cult of the saints, and urged Maria Theresa to support the Jansenist demand for the reduction of feast days.[26] Protests by the Roman curia were unavailing.[27] When Febronius, in 1763, published his *Von dem Kirchenstaat und der rechtmässigen Gewalt des Papstes,* which argued in favor of ecclesiastical collegiality, Maria Theresa was at first inclined to order the work forbidden but was dissuaded from doing so by her confessor, Provost Ignatz Müller. Thereafter the Febronians took no care to disguise their views and met regularly at the residence of Müller to discuss ways and means of reforming the church.[28] But of more direct concern is not the fact that some great men were Febronians but that many lesser ones, not as yet in the position to give open expression to their ideas, followed them.

Finally a group of Viennese Augustinians, led by Xavier Schier, must be mentioned. These men, in an attempt to break the hold of the Jesuits over the University of Vienna, launched a campaign demanding a liberalization of the curriculum under

25. Wagner, "Gallikanismus," p. 525. Perhaps the most implacable enemy of the Jesuits in Austria, Prince Kaunitz, after the dissolution of the Society in 1773, urged that individual members not be driven out of the country, but rather that their talents be used in schools, universities, missions, orphanages, etc., which suggests that he must have believed them to be not irremediably committed to a systematic obscurantism. See F. Maass, "Die österreichische Jesuiten zwischen Josephinismus und Liberalismus," *Zeitschrift für katholische Theologie,* LXXX (1958), 66.

26. Winter, *Frühaufklärung,* p. 140; Tomek, *Kirchengeschichte,* III, p. 224.

27. F. Dörrer, "Römische Stimmen zum Frühjosephinismus," *M.I.Ö.G.,* LXIII (1955), 470–476.

28. E. Winter, *Joseph II.: Von den geistigen Quellen und letzten Beweggründen seiner Reformideen* (Vienna, 1946), p. 24; F. Maass, *Der Josephinismus: Ursprung und Wesen* (5 vols., Vienna, 1951–61), II, 72–73; see also my "The Origins of Josephinism: Two Studies," *Colorado College Studies,* VII (1964), 34–35.

the slogan of a "flight from Scholasticism."[29] Here too were
trained pens, ready to express dangerous opinions if only for the
sake of doing in a hated rival. This is the place to bring up the
subject of the Austrian universities, which, it would be only
logical to assume, should have played a major role in the Austrian
enlightenment. It was, in fact, at best modest. This is usually
explained by the dead hand of the Jesuits in not allowing the
universities to participate in any debates of intellectual significance and, subsidiarily, by the contempt in which higher
education was held by Joseph II. The matter is rather more
complicated. The universities were languishing long before
Joseph began to neglect them. To give only a few examples: in
1737 the University of Vienna was relieved of its duties in the
censoring of the periodical press because there were simply not
enough professors with the necessary qualifications available;
the principal library collections in the monarchy were not univer-
sity-connected but could be found in the Gschwindiana, the
private collection of the late Field Marshal Johann Martin
Gschwind, housed in a Dominican monastery in Vienna, and in
a second private library located in Amras castle in the Tyrol;
the University of Graz was plagued with declining enrollments
throughout the century (by 1781 it could boast of no more than
twenty-two matriculants); in Vienna the faculty had been reduced to no more than twelve professors, including both *ordi-
narii* and *extraordinarii*. Nor can the parlous state of this
university be blamed entirely on the Jesuits, who in 1759 lost
the direction of theological studies and in 1765 the chair of
canon law.[30] The situation was recognized to be so serious that

29. Winter, *Frühaufklärung*, p. 145.
30. *Ibid.*, p. 111; R. Kink, *Geschichte der kaiserlichen Universität zu Wien*
(2 vols. in 3, Vienna, 1854), I/2, 235; W. Pongratz, "Geschichte der Universitätsbibliothek," *Studien zur Geschichte der Universität Wien*, I (1965), 21; F. v. Krones,
Geschichte der Karl-Franzens Universität in Graz (Graz, 1886), p. 462. See also my
Joseph II (New York, 1968), pp. 57–60; also J. Pezzl, *Beschreibung und Grundriss
der Haupt- und Residenzstadt Wien* (3rd ed., Vienna, 1809), p. 186; and A. Lhotsky,
Österreichische Historiographie (Vienna, 1962), p. 129.

in 1772 Prince Kaunitz took the unusual step of sending Johann Melchior von Birkenstock to Protestant Göttingen to report on what factors combined to produce a successful university. Birkenstock's praise of Göttingen may be read as a critique of Vienna: the professors were without exception learned men, they were well and regularly paid, and the intellectual climate was distinguished by its cosmopolitanism—there were students of all religions and nationalities, some even from distant America. Perhaps this state of affairs was regarded as utopian. No action, at any rate, was taken on the report.[31] Certainly, even in Vienna, where there was at least no shortage of students, money was woefully scarce,[32] and for this reason alone the university would have been impeded in participating in a more active way in the broader intellectual life of the monarchy.

Insofar as any formal philosophic tendency can be said to have prevailed in this rather diverse environment, the ideas of Christian Wolff were at its center. His system, derived largely from Samuel Pufendorf and Christian Thomasius and elaborated in courses of lectures at Halle and Marburg, insisted upon the unvaryingly rational and teleological nature of the universe. Within this framework he evolved a sort of ethically governed meliorism. His ideas were popularized in Austria by Heinrich Gottlieb von Justi, a professor at the Theresianum in Vienna who accomplished the considerable feat of deriving from Montesquieu arguments in support of the proposition that only absolute monarchy can solve the problems of mankind; by Paul Joseph Riegger, late of Innsbruck, who proceeded from a position based on natural law to demonstrate that the state had the right and duty to govern the church; and by Karl Anton Martini, who was willing to admit of no restraint upon the powers that might reasonably be left to the state, which was, given its varied re-

31. A. Lhotsky, "Ein Bericht über die Universität Göttingen für den Staatskanzler Fürst Kaunitz-Rietberg 1772," *Festschrift Percy Ernst Schramm* (2 vols., Wiesbaden, 1964), II, 75–78.

32. H. Demelius, "Beiträge zur Haushaltsgeschichte der Universität Wien," *Studien zur Geschichte der Universität Wien*, I (1965), 208.

sponsibilities, obliged to control the lives of its citizens even within their private residences. Agriculture, commerce, above all education were within its purview.[33] Without any doubt, the emphasis was on *étatisme* rather than on individual liberty, which may, of course, at least partly be explained by the undeniable fact that in the experience of these men only the state was able to assure the safety of the citizen or, indeed, take an interest in it.[34]

There was one other important gathering ground of actual, or at least potential, literary talent, and that was Free Masonry. It is not entirely clear when the Masons first penetrated Austria—probably sometime in the late 1720's. Having established themselves there, they were able to win over no less a figure than Francis Stephen of Lorraine, husband of Maria Theresa, Grand Duke of Tuscany, and future Holy Roman Emperor. In 1738 Clement XII issued the bull *In eminenti* condemning Masonry and all its works. Francis Stephen, to whom the question of the enforcement of the bull was referred, rendered the Solomonic judgment that, in order not to hurt the feelings of the papacy, the bull was to be published, but so long as the lodges did not call attention to themselves by undue public activity, they were not to be bothered. In 1751, when a second bull condemned the Masons, Francis Stephen was more direct. He simply prevented its publication in the Habsburg dominions.[35] With such patronage it is no wonder that the lodges not only flourished but became the meeting ground of the Viennese *grand monde*.

33. Bernard, "Origins of Josephenism," pp. 42–43; F. Valjavec, *Der Josefinismus* (2nd ed., Munich, 1945), pp. 9–10; L. Krieger, *The Politics of Discretion* (Chicago and London, 1965), pp. 263–264; H. v. Voltelini, "Die naturrechtlichen Lehren und die Reformen des 18. Jahrhunderts," *H.Z.*, CV (1910), 101–102.

34. B. v. Wiese, *Politische Dichtung Deutschlands* (Berlin, 1931), p. 28. Ultimately there evolved what has with some justice been called "la véritable idolatrie de l'État." See R. Bauer, "Le Joséphisme," *Critique*, XI (1958), 639.

35. G. Kuéss and B. Scheichelbauer, *200 Jahre Freimaurerei in Österreich* (Vienna, 1959), p. 13; F. J. Schneider, *Die Freimaurerei und ihr Einfluss auf die geistige Kultur in Deutschland am Ende des 18. Jahrhunderts* (Prague, 1909), p. 39. For Francis Stephen see F. Hennings, *Und sitzet zur linken Hand: Franz Stephan von Lothringen* (Vienna, Berlin, and Stuttgart, 1961).

Whereas in France Masonry had assumed an unmistakable anti-aristocratic tone—at least aristocracy of birth was continually denounced—in Austria the flower of the nobility regularly could be found in the lodges on meeting nights. The rosters boasted such names as Bathyany, Bethlen, Draskovic, Hoyos, Kaunitz, Paar, Schwarzenberg, Trauttmansdorff, and Windischgrätz. Doubtless of some symbolic importance was that, contrary to the practice in the English lodges, where upon entering all members divested themselves of their swords, the practice in Germany and Austria was for the bourgeois members to be girt with swords as they came in. Equality was thus achieved on the nobiliar level. In spite of this, the men who directed the Austrian lodges did not belong to these august circles, but were either, like Ignatz von Born and Tobias von Gebler, members of the lower aristocracy, or, like the jurist Paul Joseph Riegger, belonged to the bourgeoisie.[36]

We shall have occasion to return to the subject of Free Masonry when we discuss the careers of various prominent writers of the Austrian enlightenment. At this point it would be well to observe that to attribute to it, as some critics of the enlightenment have done, the sole responsibility for marshaling the forces inimical to the religious or to the political establishment is both simplistic and naive. Within the confines of the monarchy there were dozens of lodges with hundreds of members who took the most diverse positions on the great questions of the day; every position on the political spectrum was represented in them. And as Joseph II remained throughout his life distantly cool to Ma-

---

36. Kuéss and Scheichelbauer, *200 Jahre Freimaurerei*, p. 19; B. Faÿ, *La Franc-Maçonnerie et la révolution intellectuelle du 18e siècle* (2nd ed., Paris, 1961), pp. 184–189; L. Abafi, *Geschichte der Freimaurerei in Oesterreich-Ungarn* (5 vols., Budapest, 1890–97), I, 148–151; H. Boos, *Geschichte der Freimaurerei* (2nd ed., Aarau, 1906), p. 231. It may be of significance that whereas in the German polemical literature of the second half of the eighteenth century aristocrats are generally portrayed in the worst possible light, appearing as libertines, slaves to their base passions and the like, one does not find such denunciations of the nobility in Austria. See E. Sauer, *Die französische Revolution von 1789 in zeitgenössischen deutschen Flugschriften und Dichtungen* (Weimar, 1913), p. 5.

sonry, there is really no reason at all to represent either the Josephinian reforms or the Austrian enlightenment as a Masonic conspiracy.[37] The lodges were merely a convenient place for young writers to read their work to an appreciative audience and to be reassured by the benevolent presence of the great.

There was not much in the way of a strict literary tradition. The Austrian baroque had not produced many writers of note. The best known, perhaps, were Wolfgang von Hohberg, who produced a massive epic poem in alexandrines, *Der Habsburgische Ottobert*, hardly distinguishable from similar works written in the late Middle Ages, and *Georgica curiosa*, which contained much useful information for the rural squire as well as some sharply observed vignettes of rural life;[38] and Catherina Regina von Greiffenberg, who wrote a series of touching appeals for religious toleration and for an increase in godliness.[39] Both of these writers were Protestants and were forced to spend their declining years in exile in Germany. Their imitators in the first half of the eighteenth century are most charitably passed over in silence. Suffice it to say that the Jesuitical-bardic poetry that they produced reached the nadirs of both genres.[40] Apart from this, there is really only the curious, contorted, sometimes brilliant, always idiosyncratic oeuvre of Abraham à Sancta Clara.[41]

37. In 1776 a Danish captain, von Sudthausen, in Vienna on a diplomatic mission, made a determined attempt to win Joseph over for Masonry. After initially appearing interested, the Emperor replied that he could not possibly join a society whose constitution was secret and thus unknown to him, and stubbornly refused all of Sudthausen's attempts to have the mysteries revealed to him, as it were, ex officio. See E. Lennhoff, *Die Freimaurer* (2nd ed., Zürich, Leipzig, and Vienna, 1929), pp. 179–181.

38. Kann, *Austrian Intellectual History*, p. 39; Nadler, *Literaturgeschichte*, pp. 133–134.

39. Nadler, *Literaturgeschichte*, pp. 134–135; H. J. Frank, *Catherina Regina von Greiffenberg* (Göttingen, 1967), pp. 36–44.

40. Harsh as this judgment seems, it is also inescapable. The man who without doubt was most familiar with Austrian literature of the eighteenth century, Gustav Gugitz, speaks of "empty formalism" and the "pedantic dilettantism of the Jesuits." See his "Die Wiener Stubenmädchenlitteratur von 1781," *Zeitschrift für Bücherfreunde*, VI/1 (1902), 137.

41. For a sensitive appreciation of Abraham, see Kann, *Austrian Intellectual*

He found hardly any imitators, in spite of the fact that his work can be regarded as a summation of the baroque era.

Part of the difficulty undoubtedly was the considerable gulf that had come to separate spoken from written German in Austria. It could be argued that Austrian writers were from the outset handicapped by having to write in a language which they did not really use in their daily lives. Gottsched, always anxious to be helpful, offered to supervise a general purification of spoken Austro-German, an offer which, much to his surprise, was indignantly rejected. More practically, the Slovene Johann Popovič, first in Kremsmünster, then in Vienna, attempted to arrive at a compromise by systematizing some of the dialects common in Austria.[42] His system might ultimately have produced a generation capable of expressing itself gramatically in Austro-German, but on the whole it is probably fortunate that, in the event, Austrian letters did not have to wait upon the maturation of these specially trained schoolboys.

We have already noted the fact that a change in atmosphere becomes perceptible, if at first only slowly, after the middle of the century. In spite of official disapproval, the Theresan reforms brought with them a change in taste. Klopstock, Gellert, and Lessing were beginning to be read in Austria. The Jesuit bards began to fade into a much-deserved oblivion. One of the most notorious of them, Michael Denis, in 1762 strode out in a new direction by publishing an anthology meant to introduce the youth of Austria to the better-known German poets. In the same year, the ex-Saxon Christian Gottlob Klemm began to publish the first Viennese literary review, *Die Welt*.[43] These were only straws in the wind, but unmistakable ones.

History, pp. 50–115. He makes a convincing case for the proposition that Abraham's only successor in Austria was Karl Lueger at the end of the nineteenth century.

42. Nadler, *Literaturgeschichte*, p. 181; Winter, *Frühaufklärung*, p. 144.

43. Fischer-Colbrie, *Michael Denis*, p. 6; Mühlher, "Literatur der Aufklärung," p. 291; G. Gugitz, *Das Wertherfieber in Oesterreich* (Vienna, 1908), p. iv; E. V.

This on-the-surface unpromising literary constellation has been variously interpreted. It has, for instance, been suggested that an extremely tyrannical reactionary regime allied to archaic feudal interests refused to allow the genuinely creative, potentially materialist strain among physicians, preachers, teachers, publicists, bureaucrats, and even merchants to develop and find its voice, and that not only the pervasive mediocrity of the period but also its characteristic tensions can be explained in these terms.[44] Or, that because of the separation of the two German cultural spheres already alluded to, Austria did not participate in the Klopstockian break with the cold, mechanistic literature of the seventeenth century, and thus, instead of participating in the ever-widening exploration of the subjective life of the soul, Austrian literature, still basically a court literature, addressed itself to an ever-narrower audience whose onetime humanistic interests had been frozen into heartless self-interest. From this trap escape was possible only through a bourgeois-oriented return to pietism, the way being shown by such works as *Robinson Crusoe*. In contrast, Germany did not lack its court culture: its despots were ready to interfere with any sign of an undue interest in questions best left to them. They were, however, powerless to interfere with the enlightenment, as, for the most part, it proceeded on its work in the free cities not subject to despotic control.[45] Or yet, that the underlying tension between a mechanistically determined cosmology inherited from the seventeenth century and the ever-stronger stirrings of human fantasy typical of the eighteenth could only be resolved by a genuine

Zenker, "Geschichte des Wiener Zeitungswesens von seinem Anfängen bis zum Jahre 1800," *Ö.U.R.*, n.F., X (1891), 301.

44. A. W. Gulyga, *Der deutsche Materialismus am Ausgang des 18. Jahrhunderts*, trans. I. Bauer and G. Korf (Berlin, 1966), pp. 11–12; G. Stiehler, *Beiträge zur Geschichte des vormarxistischen Materialismus* (Berlin, 1961).

45. F. Bruggemann, "Der Kampf um die bürgerliche Welt- und Lebensanschaung in der deutschen Literatur des 18. Jahrhunderts," *D.V.L.G.*, III/1 (1925), 96–98; W. Krauss, *Die französische Aufklärung im Spiegel der deutschen Literatur des 18. Jahrhunderts* (Berlin, 1963), pp. lxxiv–lxxvi.

synthesis of the scientific spirit with the artistic impulse—the preconditions for which were obviously not present in Austria—or by a headlong flight into completely unfettered fantasy. Along this road the temptations to give way to obscurantism are both obvious and frequent.[46]

One may make what one wishes of these analyses. It does seem that no such complicated and class-oriented structures are necessary to interpret the scene under review. It appears to be beyond dispute that for a variety of reasons Austria for a time was cut off from some, but not all, of the dominant intellectual tendencies of the West; that as a result the intelligentsia underwent a somewhat unusual grouping, which in itself would be sufficient explantation for any appearances of class cohesion; and that for essentially political reasons there was a considerable effort made after the middle of the century to achieve a juncture with the West, which, in spite of continuing official disapproval, brought about an intellectual revival.[47] This explanation is sufficient to account both for the existence of an Austrian intelligentsia at the beginning of the 1760's and for its varying outlooks. We must now examine the conditions under which these men were to write.

In Austria, as in most other countries at the time, what men would have chosen to write was not always identical with what they wrote. The difference was accounted for by the existence of censorship. That, in itself, was nothing remarkable. Of all the countries of Europe only England and, by extension, Hanover did not engage heavily in the censorship of literature. All writers knew how to operate within these limits. The great thing was to work under a censorship that was not wholly oppressive, that

---

46. Mühlher, "Literatur der Aufklärung," pp. 284–285.

47. This is the opinion of most writers on the subject, with the notable exception of Catholic apologists, who sometimes go so far as to argue that whereas German literature experienced a revival, in Austria there was a retrograde movement which saw letters hopelessly mired in mud and filth. See C. Wolfsgruber, *Christian Anton Kardinal Migazzi* (Ravensburg, 1897), p. 577.

could be outwitted if not actually evaded. Censorship in the Habsburg dominions was first introduced systematically in the course of the struggle against Protestantism. A decree of November, 1559, turned over to the University of Vienna—and thus in practical terms to the Jesuits—the responsibility for examining all imported books for evidences of heresy, and shortly thereafter it was charged with examining domestic literature as well. This situation still obtained at the beginning of the eighteenth century, when, in the brief reign of Joseph I, a somewhat more liberal policy was followed. Among other arguments, the Emperor advanced the proposition that books with a mainly political content should be passed on by governmental, not clerical, censors. This procedure actually survived the period of reaction that set in after Joseph's early death in 1711, but in all other respects the censorship reverted to its long-accustomed severity. Not only books tainted by Protestant arguments but books by Protestants on any subject whatever were burned wherever they were found. The accession of Maria Theresa in 1740 at first threatened to make an already bad situation even worse as the young Jesuit-educated Archduchess, pious to a fault even in her youth, turned back to the Jesuits full control over even political literature, a decision which was, however, reversed in 1743, largely because the university could not keep up with the work. By 1749 Maria Theresa, although no less pious, had been sufficiently convinced of the utility of employing capable servants in all sectors of the administration to inquire of the *Directorium in Publicis et Cameralibus* (the equivalent of a Ministry for Internal Affairs) what steps should be undertaken with respect to reforming the censorship. The result of the exchange which followed, in conjunction with the general administrative reform of that year, was the creation of a Censorship Commission. At first the differences were minimal. The president of the commission, Count Schrattenbach, favored the Jesuit position: booksellers were hauled into court for offering for sale copies of the

Esprit des lois, and although the establishment of an Austrian *Catalogum librorum prohibitorum* in 1752 may be regarded as an attempt on the part of the liberals to put at least some limit on the number of books condemned by the commission, the *Catalogum* soon grew very fat. It was not until 1759 that the Jesuits went too far. They attempted to restructure the commission without first consulting the highest authority, and the liberals were now able to convince Maria Theresa that her powers were being challenged. This led to a considerable shake-up.[48] After 1759 the commission was made up of four secular and three ecclesiastical members, under the presidency of Gerhard van Swieten, the noted Dutch physician who in 1745 had accepted an invitation to come to Vienna in order to reform the university in general and the teaching of medicine in particular. The other secular members were Martini, an obscure professor of Greek named Gasparri, and the editor of the semi-official *Wiener Tagblatt,* a man named Gontier. The clerical members were Simon Stock and two canons named Semmen and Girtler.[49]

As van Swieten and Stock were Jansenists, and Martini was obsessed with the necessity of establishing the control of state over church, it was hardly surprising that the concerns of the censorship would now be somewhat changed. The charge under which the commission operated instructed it to ban three categories of works: those inveighing against the faith, those endangering the public weal or the interests of the monarch, and all those offending against good morals. The charge was broad, but could be variously interpreted. As it turned out, only with respect to the third category did the commission remain as in-

---

48. Bernard, "Origins of Josephinism," p. 9; A. Fournier, "Gerhard van Swieten als Censor," *Sitzungsberichte der Kaiserlichen Akademie der Wissenschaften, Philosophisch-historische Classe,* LXXXIV (1876), 391–405; F. H. Meyer, "Zur Geschichte der österreichischen Bücherpolizei," *Archiv für Geschichte des deutschen Buchhandels,* XIV (1891), 366–370. On the reform of 1749 see F. Walter, *Die Theresianische Staatsreform von 1749* (Vienna, 1958).

49. W. Müller, *Gerhard van Swieten* (Vienna, 1883), pp. 119–134; A. Ellemunter, *Antonio Eugenio Visconti und die Anfänge des Josephinismus* (Graz and Cologne, 1963), pp. 40–41.

flexible as its Jesuit predecessors.[50] Such works as Christoph Martin Wieland's *Agathon* and Friedrich Schiller's *Die Räuber* were rejected as immoral, as was, at a lower level, Josef Kurzbock's *Beyträge zur Schilderung Wiens*, which, it was held, was too graphic in its descriptions of the activities of the Viennese *belles de la nuit*, activities which were, however, tolerated by the police.

Works dangerous to the Catholic religion were now, in general, regarded much more tolerantly. This seems to have been not merely the result of the Jansenists wishing to secure the circulation of works favorable to their cause, but also part of a concerted and systematic attempt on the part of the state chancellor, Prince Kaunitz, to remove all secular power from ecclesiastical hands. Thus, perforce, the power to object to published works had to be included.[51] Still, the censorship was unpredictable, and it was possible to go too far in attacking religion. The condemnation of Joseph von Sonnenfels' *Der Mann ohne Vorurteil* is a case in point. The archbishop of Vienna, Cardinal Migazzi, in 1767 protested directly to Maria Theresa about the objectionable content of this publication, comparing it to the worst excesses of Luther and Calvin, and the Empress not only ordered it to be banned, but upbraided the Censorship Commission for having passed it in the first place.[52] As late as 1781 Lessing's *Von dem Zwecke Jesu und seiner Jünger* was banned as insulting to the Catholic religion.[53] Attacking religion was a lottery, in which the odds were noticeably shifting in favor of the bold pens. But it was always possible to come up a loser at the most unexpected time.

50. Müller, *Gerhard van Swieten*, p. 119; F. Walter, "Die zensurierten Klassiker," *J.G.G.*, XXIX (1930), 140; Th. Wiedemann, "Die kirchliche Bücher-Censur in der Erzdiöcese Wien," *A.Ö.G.*, L (1873), 319.

51. Ellemunter, *A. E. Visconti*, p. 43; Maass, *Der Josephinismus*, I, 56; Maass, "Vorbereitung und Anfänge des Josephinismus," *M.Ö.S.*, I/2 (1948), 299.

52. Wiedemann, "Bücher-Censur," pp. 296–299. For a detailed discussion of Sonnenfels and his journal, see the next chapter.

53. Walter, "Klassiker," p. 146.

In matters concerning the public interest and the governance of the realm it becomes difficult to generalize about the Austrian censorship, which on this plane seemed to proceed in two almost contrary directions. On the one hand, the governing principle seemed to be "dass sich Privati in Händel der Souveräne gar nicht, viel weniger mit etwas spitzen Ausdrücken mischen sollen." In other words, the actions of the government were not to be commented on in print, as it turned out, either favorably or unfavorably. Maria Theresa insisted upon the suppression of Sonnenfels' weekly *Der Vertraute* after only seven issues had appeared because it had dared to attack the persons of certain high aristocrats for their reactionary tendencies and had defended actions taken against them by the crown.[54] Yet from the beginning of his co-regency in 1765, Joseph was to argue for at least a partial liberalization of the censorship in this area. In a long memorandum written in that year, he maintained that while great care had to be exercised in deciding what should be allowed to appear in print, one must beware of an excess of zeal, particularly where the persons of foreigners were concerned. Man's inborn liberty ought not to be denied him, except of course in cases where the interests of the state were directly involved. There a blind identification with the sovereign's opinion was demanded of the subject. Still, one ought not to ignore the sad fact that every single book banned by the censorship was easily available in Vienna.[55] While Joseph's reservations about the freedom of the press seemed clear enough to him, the whole statement was sufficiently equivocal to allow for a wide latitude of interpretations. In practice, the Censorship Commission in the period 1765–72 followed the lead of men like Riegger and Justi, who argued for a rather more latitudinarian view of political

54. Fournier, "Gerhard van Swieten," pp. 427–428; H. Gnau, *Die Zensur unter Joseph II.* (Strasbourg and Leipzig, 1911), p. 56.

55. A. v. Arneth, *Maria Theresia und Joseph II.: Ihre Correspondenz* (3 vols., Vienna, 1867–68), III, 352.

literature. In 1772, with the death of van Swieten, the commission fell apart. Semmen, Gontier, Stock, and Sonnenfels, who had in the meantime been added to it, resigned, and Martini all but ceased to function as a member. A man named von Koch became president and his new colleagues were men as obscure as he.[56] One important consequence of this change, though, was that Sonnenfels was followed as the censor responsible for the theater by Franz Carl Hägelin. Sonnenfels had broken many a lance on behalf of classical drama and against the popular form of Viennese comedy, the *Hanswurst*, but Hägelin was a thorough obscurantist as well as a master of trivial persecution. He refused to allow not only the least indication of immorality on the stage (male and female characters were not permitted to make simultaneous exits lest the audience suspect that they were off to an assignation) but also blue-penciled everything that seemed even remotely ideological. It is due to his zeal as much as to anything else that the Viennese theater, by far the most popular literary form, remained relatively free of any major radical tendency.

Hereafter, until Joseph's new censorship law passed after Maria Theresa's death, political literature was allowed or forbidden essentially according to how the commissioners interpreted what the Emperor's attitude toward a certain work might be, with the possibility always present that Maria Theresa might interfere. Joseph's position was essentially that the person of the monarch was, while above the struggle, by no means sacred, but that the state, in encompassing the common good, must not be criticized. In practice, he was willing to allow discussions of politics, administrative concerns, military affairs, and judicial matters in longer works written by scholars, but not in the periodical press, destined to be read by the common people.[57] This,

---

56. Fournier, "Gerhard van Swieten," pp. 405, 445; Müller, *Gerhard van Swieten*, pp. 144–145; H. Rieder, *Wiener Vormärz* (Vienna, 1959), p. 36.

57. Gnau, *Die Zensur*, p. 66; O. Sashegyi, *Zensur und Geistesfreiheit unter Joseph II.* (Budapest, 1958), p. 12.

with one significant exception, the case of Sonnenfels and the *Mann ohne Vorurteil* to be discussed shortly, was where matters stood throughout the co-regency.

If, then, the loosening of the censorship was anything but complete, and it would still take a reckless man to express views radically different from the norm, at least cracks were appearing. And there can be no question that the volume of publications increased significantly. It is known, for instance, that in 1773 the total monetary value of all books exported from Austria was 135,000 florins. A decade later this amount had increased to just over 3,250,000 florins.[58] And the more literature that appeared, the greater the burdens put upon already overworked censors and the better the chance for the occasional radical piece to get by.

Finally, it will be necessary to say a few words about the available outlets for publication. Up until the middle of the eighteenth century there was hardly an establishment in Austria worthy of the name of publishing house. There were numerous printers, of course, most of them in Vienna, but even though some of them made a reasonable living by working on government commissions or printing plays, not one had made even a modest fortune. Yet, for those with eyes to see, there was money to be made. Although there was no such thing as a generally recognized copyright before the nineteenth century, privileges for specific printings, accorded by royal or other authority, did to some extent protect from bald theft the texts of works appearing in print. But these privileges were not honored everywhere, and in the seventeenth century the Netherlands and Switzerland emerged as the recognized centers of book piracy.[59] Privileges were rigidly observed throughout Germany, but after the turn

58. J. G. I. Breitkopf, "Ueber Buchdruckerey und Buchhandel in Leipzig," *Journal für Fabrik. Manufaktur und Handlung*, V (1793), 30.

59. *Ibid.*, p. 51; J. Nadler, *Buchhandel, Literatur und Nation in Geschichte und Gegenwart* (Berlin, 1932), p. 23. The first privilege accorded to a printer is thought to have been issued in Venice in 1469.

of the century, partly as a result of Hörnigk's Cameralist doctrines, prohibitions against the reprinting of books, or *Nachdruck*, were no longer enforced in Austria. Because of the peculiar nature of the censorship, moreover, it was much more difficult to import books from Protestant Germany, which works suspicious customs officials tended to exclude on principle, than to print precisely the same things in Austria. Thus there was a double opportunity for those with sufficient vision and a corresponding lack of scruple: it was possible to print cheaply, as no royalties would have to be paid to the publishers and authors whose works were being pirated; and by reprinting materials that were known to have been excluded by the customs, one could appeal to a variety of prurient interests.[60]

Under such circumstances it was hardly possible not to make a fortune, and the first man to recognize this would become very rich indeed. He was, in fact, the son of an unsuccessful Hungarian miller, Joseph Thomas Trattner. In 1748 he borrowed 4,000 florins and bought a small printing establishment in Vienna. He succeeded in ingratiating himself with van Swieten, and through that powerful man's influence was accorded the position of *Privilegierter Hofdrucker*, which meant that he had a guaranteed amount of commissions from the court. His work seems to have been satisfactory, as in 1751 he was given practically the whole of the court trade. Profits from this business enabled him to open his own bookshop a year later. In 1755, more in the hope of making even more money than in order to provide an outlet for the local literati, he founded the *Wienerische gelehrten Nachrichten*. But either there were too few scholars to justify regular accounts of their activities, or the reading public was not sufficiently curious, and after appearing sporadically for two or three years, the paper quietly folded. Trattner was again singled out in 1756 when Archduke Joseph, who, like all the male chil-

60. Nadler, *Buchhandel*, p. 23; J. Goldfriedrich, *Geschichte des deutschen Buchhandels: 1740–1804* (Leipzig, 1909), p. 4.

dren of Francis Stephen and Maria Theresa, was to be taught a trade, was sent to his establishment to learn printing. Secure in the knowledge that he was in the good graces of the court, and sensing a change in the wind, Trattner now felt that he could begin to take risks. He began to reprint foreign books. At first he stuck to unexceptionable classics; later he pirated anything that came to hand. Within a decade he was a multimillionaire.[61]

Trattner, in part because of his semi-official position as court printer, in part because of the very magnitude of his success, came close to achieving a monopoly position in Austrian publishing. But there were areas into which he was unwilling to expand, and into these others soon moved. A moderately successful engraver and art dealer named Löschenkohl found that his engravings depicting the great or at least notorious events of the day, or the great figures of the past, sold better if they were accompanied by a text, and began pirating the north German weeklies.[62] Often his hastily prepared publications did not contain sufficient material to fill out their pages. Rather than to leave these blank, Löschenkohl resorted to publishing whatever came to hand: miserable doggerel, stanzas from the Ancients, or even occasional pieces written by local talent. In many ways his business operations prefigured those of the rather better-known Georg Philipp Wucherer, who was to become notorious in the 1780's. The activities of Trattner and his lesser imitators were, at best, morally dubious. It may even be, as Sonnenfels objected in 1765, that by flooding the country with north German literature they were inhibiting the development of an equivalent Austrian school. Such a judgment, however, is too narrowly mercantilistic. The pirate-publishers performed two important functions: they brought the bulk of the German enlightenment

61. Goldfriedrich, *Deutschen Buchhandels*, pp. 5–7; Abafi, *Freimaurerei*, I, 154; J. Mentschl and G. Otruba, *Österreichische Industrielle und Bankiers* (Vienna, 1965), p. 36.

62. K. Schottenloher, *Flugblatt und Zeitung* (Berlin, 1922), pp. 331–334.

to Austria, and, although they paid miserably, they did provide Austrian writers, if not with the opportunity to make a living with their pens, at least with the chance to be published. This made it possible for Austria to have an enlightenment of its own.

2

The First Radical: Joseph von Sonnenfels

ON AUGUST 18, 1765, Emperor Francis Stephen died suddenly in Innsbruck, where he had gone for the wedding of his second son Leopold. His death indirectly brought about the first major opportunity for the more advanced sort of enlightened opinion to be heard in Austria. In the aftermath of the Seven Years' War the Austrian government had been faced with the sad but inescapable realization that not only had the great reform of 1749 not resulted in the hoped-for recovery of Silesia, but it had not even succeeded in achieving an acceptable level of increase in the marshaling of the monarchy's resources. Another major effort was obviously indicated. Working in the main with the newly created *Staatsrat,* Maria Theresa and Prince Kaunitz in 1764 and 1765 attempted to realize those aspects of the great Haugwitzian reform program that had, through neglect and the opposition of entrenched interests, remained dead letters. This is not the place to launch into a detailed description of the Theresan reforms. Suffice it to say that the atmosphere of those years, in spite of the recently unhappily concluded war, was one of considerable optimism and confidence that fairly comprehensive changes were in the immediate offing.[1] It is no

1. E. Guglia, *Maria Theresia* (2 vols., Munich and Berlin, 1917), II, 174–175; P. Müller, "Der aufgeklärte Absolutismus in Österreich," *Bulletin of the International Committee of Historical Sciences,* IX/1 (1937), 25–28.

wonder that those with advanced ideas were encouraged to believe that the time had come to air them, and that the Censorship Commission proceeded with greater reticence than formerly in the assessment of questionable literature.

This, then, was the situation at the Emperor's death. Maria Theresa's reaction to the loss of her husband was initially one of near collapse. She withdrew into her grief, let it be known that she no longer wished to concern herself with affairs of state, and talked about retiring to a nunnery. It was generally assumed that Archduke Joseph, who was presently proclaimed co-regent in place of his father, would soon be ruling alone. In view of his somewhat undeserved reputation for holding liberal opinions, it was also entirely reasonable that the liberals should feel encouraged. In the event, Maria Theresa, dissuaded from abdicating by Kaunitz, did not do so, but, at least in her first year of widowhood, she gave way to her grief to such an extent that it would be only somewhat hyperbolic to speak of an interregnum.[2] Joseph, who immediately after his father's death had made the tactical mistake of letting it be known that he proposed to introduce vast changes at all levels of government, was kept from exercising any real power, and the government ran itself as best it could. So in 1765 and 1766 it was possible in Austria to do as one pleased to a vastly greater extent than at any time in the past, and for some time in the future.

We have already noted that in 1762 Christian Gottlob Klemm had tried his luck at publishing a weekly, *Die Welt*, in Vienna. This soon failed, but two years later he tried once more with *Der österreichische Patriot*. This publication, like the former, was careful not to antagonize the censorship and did not venture out on the treacherous ground of political commentary, but Klemm as a good Gottschedian broke many a lance in favor of the German language and against the primacy of foreign influences. In the course of developing this argument, as it were *en passant*, Klemm delivered himself of a series of sharp attacks on

2. Bernard, *Joseph II*, pp. 31–35.

the Austrian nobility, which, he said, aped foreign manners to the extent that it was no longer able to express itself correctly in its native language.[3] This accusation was not only generally accurate but also relatively safe to make in view of Joseph's already well-known tendency to favor the German language. It passed unchallenged, and so may be considered the entering wedge for a more ambitious attack on the aristocracy in particular and the social order in general. But the man who was to make that attack was not Klemm but Joseph von Sonnenfels.

Sonnenfels was the grandson of the chief rabbi of Brandenburg. His father emigrated to Austria, first to the Burgenland, then to Moravia. His activities as a Hebrew scholar brought him to the attention first of the Piarist fathers and then of the feudal magnate of the region, Prince Dietrichstein. Sometime after 1736 he was converted to Catholicism and assumed the name of Alois Wiener. His new faith opened up to him a career appropriate to his talents, and in 1745 he became professor of Oriental languages at the University of Vienna. In the following year, for reasons which are not clear, as his position was hardly of an eminence to justify such a step, he was given a patent of nobility and took the name of von Sonnenfels. Joseph was born in 1732, thus as a Jew. He was baptized soon after his father's conversion, although his mother was not. He was educated first at the Piarist college in Nikolsburg, then at the University of Vienna, where he learned something of the classics and of German literature, but not French, the sine qua non for a career as an intellectual. In 1749, for reasons which are again unknown, he took the somewhat unusual step of enlisting as a common soldier in the *Deutschmeister* regiment. The conditions of his service were rather undemanding for someone with his intellectual abilities, and in five years in the army he found time to learn French, Italian, and Czech and to school himself as a writer of German. In 1754 he

3. Abafi, *Freimaurerei*, I, 134–136; Mühlher, "Literatur der Aufklärung," p. 291; Guglia, *Maria Theresia*, II, 224. Klemm's first job in Vienna was as a proofreader in Trattner's printing establishment.

obtained his discharge from the army and returned to his studies in Vienna. He attended mainly lectures in law, canon as well as civil, and was influenced by the lectures of Martini and Riegger. Beginning in 1756 he undertook the practice of law, eking out his income by means of a bookkeeper's position in a Viennese guards regiment. In 1761 he became president of a would-be literary society, the *Deutsche Gesellschaft*. All the while he read, honed his mind, and worked at improving his command of written German prose. In 1762 he deemed himself ready for undertaking larger tasks, and made an application for the chair of German literature at the University of Vienna. Since the chair was at the moment occupied, his application was unsuccessful, but perhaps in order not to disappoint him unduly, or because his position in the society had earned him something of a reputation, in the next year the government offered him the newly created chair of *Polizei- und Kameralwissenschaften*. Sonnenfels accepted and so became the first professor at Vienna of what might best be translated as political economy.[4]

Sonnenfels lost no time in establishing himself as an enfant terrible. His inaugural lecture, on the dangers of relying on the tried and true, was enough to give him the reputation of a potentially dangerous reformer.[5] In subsequent lectures he expanded on the proposition that the highest purpose of the state was to assure the welfare of its citizens. This may have been a Rousseauan position, but as it also corresponded to the view of responsible absolutism that Joseph held, this at least did him no

4. Kann, *Austrian Intellectual History*, pp. 146–154. Kann's long chapter on Sonnenfels is the best modern treatment of the subject. See also W. Müller, *Josef von Sonnenfels* (Vienna, 1882), pp. 7–11. Müller's book is the only full-scale biography, but does not meet demanding scholarly standards. Sonnenfels' appointment to his professorship was in large measure due to the influence of Baron Valerian Borié, a leading liberal in the government service. K. H. Osterloh's *Joseph von Sonnenfels und die österreichische Reformbewegung im Zeitalter des aufgeklärten Absolutismus* (Lübeck and Hamburg, 1970), in spite of its title, deals almost exclusively with Sonnenfels as administrator and administrative theoretician.

5. G. Deutsch, "Joseph v. Sonnenfels und seine Schüler," *Ö.U.R.*, n.F., V (1888), 72.

harm in that quarter. In practical terms, he maintained, the best way to promote the welfare of the population was to assist it to increase. This would eventually lead, by increasing the pressure of social needs, to a corresponding increase in production, which would result in everyone's needs being satisfied.[6] Populationism was also a favorite subject not only of Joseph's but of Maria Theresa's as well. Thus, while alienating most of his colleagues at the university, Sonnenfels was able to secure for himself potential support at court by keeping a weather eye on the atmosphere. Maria Theresa undoubtedly disapproved of his more daring flights into Rousseauism, but she was willing to accord him at least a limited freedom to criticize.[7]

A man of Sonnenfels' broad interests and dynamic energy was bound to be caught up in the rage for weekly journalism that had seized Vienna. His first venture into publishing was *Der Vertraute*, which, as has already been noted, was banned after only seven issues. But in 1765 Sonnenfels was encouraged to try again with *Der Mann ohne Vorurteil*, which was to become easily the most successful of the *Wochenschriften*. The first three issues were innocuous. In the fourth Sonnenfels decided to take some risks. He soon found that the more daring his sorties, the more his publication was bought up by a reading public which apparently wanted to hear precisely what he was telling it, and that unaccountably the censorship remained unheard from. Beginning with a Rousseauism that combined the notions of the social contract with those of the natural savage, with liberal admixtures of the educational theories of *Émile*, Sonnenfels proceeded to attack the pretensions of the parvenus of the aristocratic world, those who, like himself, had only in recent times been ennobled. This was still a relatively safe target. When nothing untoward happened, he was emboldened to take on the

6. Müller, *Josef von Sonnenfels*, p. 111.

7. Kann, *Austrian Intellectual History*, p. 159. See also C. v. Wurzbach, *Biographisches Lexicon des Kaiserthums Oesterreich* (60 vols., Vienna, 1856–91), XXXV, 317–328.

ancient nobility, and finally to address himself to what was in his mind the key question, the relations between noble land-owners and their peasants.[8] It is with the first year and a half of the *Mann ohne Vorurteil* that we will now concern ourselves in some detail.

In the fourth issue Sonnenfels introduced the technique with which he would proceed to utter the most controversial opinions while, if necessary, being able to claim that they were not really his. A savage, Capa-kaum, having been forced to leave his homeland, reaches Vienna after many vicissitudes. There he is taken in hand by some helpful gentlemen of the town who undertake to explain the local customs to him. As a literary de-vice, the transplanted savage was hardly new. Rousseau had in-vented him as a theoretical standard of comparison, and Voltaire in the *Ingénu* had brought him physically to Europe for the pur-pose of mocking his surroundings. He provided a convenient way to arrive at commentaries on society based on theoretical con-siderations rather than on close observation. As a literary persona he lacked much in verisimilitude because none of the writers who resorted to him could forbear putting words into his mouth which were incompatible with the background assigned to him, but he was certainly the fashion.[9]

Back, however, to Capa-kaum. Newly arrived in Vienna, he finds that he cannot sleep at night because of the continual rois-tering of his neighbors. He is told that they are people of quality who, having to spend their days working for the welfare of their less fortunate fellow citizens, must restore their energies at night.[10] When he also objects to the strange cries coming up from the street at intervals, he is told about night watchmen,

---

8. For critiques of Sonnenfels as journalist, see Kann, *Austrian Intellectual History*, pp. 196–200; E. V. Zenker, *Geschichte der Wiener Journalistik von den Anfängen bis zum Jahre 1848* (Vienna and Leipzig, 1892), pp. 50–51; and Nagl, Zeidler, and Castle, *Literaturgeschichte*, II, 285–287.

9. M. Lederer, "Die Gestalt des Naturkindes im 18. Jahrhundert," *Programm der K. K. Staats-Oberrealschule in Bielitz*, XXXII (1908), 10–15.

10. J. v. Sonnenfels, *Gesammelte Schriften* (10 vols., Vienna, 1783–87), I, 135.

which leads him to observe that it is passing strange that an occupation which requires so great a trust should be so poorly paid.[11] At this point Capa-kaum disappears momentarily from view, to be replaced by straightforward and theoretical disquisitions. There is an attack on a noble seducer,[12] a piece making fun of the quarrels over precedence which were so frequently the accompaniment of aristocratic life,[13] and then the misadventures of Sir Thomas Varnish, a young English lord, a parvenu, who in addition has inherited far more money than is good for him, are related.[14] All of these pieces are interspersed among others which deal with purely literary subjects, or are of an otherwise politically harmless nature. There now follows a classical fable. Tirin, having been created a count, visits his old father Palomon. The old man, who lives very simply, admonishes his son not to allow himself to be blinded by appearances. Merit should be the only road to advancement and favor.[15] This in turn is followed by another fable about Alcindor, a man both rich and powerful, who, however, refuses to admit that he is obligated to serve the society that has permitted him to reach his great eminence. In a coda it is pointed out that laws were made precisely for the purpose of controlling the excesses of people like him.[16]

At intervals, again with an eye on the censorship, Sonnenfels printed purported letters from outraged readers, objecting to his positions and setting out contrary ones. This had the further advantage of providing him with straw men to knock down at will. In one such reply he defends the right of Capa-kaum to criticize his hosts. This might offend against the responsibilities of accepting hospitality, but these disappear before more immediate and important considerations. Indeed, the whole concept of the essential benevolence of society is called into ques-

11. *Ibid.*, p. 140.
12. *Ibid.*, p. 180.
13. *Ibid.*, p. 222.
14. *Ibid.*, pp. 258ff.
15. *Ibid.*, pp. 325ff.
16. *Ibid.*, II, 24ff.

tion when an observer, mere savage though he be, sees on the one hand plenty, waste, and pride, and on the other scarcity, enforced economies, and the need to demean oneself. It will be hard to convince him that the man who is driven by in a gilded carriage and the other who by his own exertions drags a heavy barrow, the man for whom four cooks work all day and the other who is happy to have a piece of bread to eat at noon, the man protected from the rigors of winter by Siberian furs and the other who freezes on the street in his rags—that both men partake to the same extent of the gifts society has to offer.[17] This passage is remarkable not only because it seems strangely out of context—Capa-kaum has made no observations so far which even remotely resemble these in their sharpness—but because it speaks a language that has hardly been heard in Austria before.

Capa-kaum now returns and begins to ask some very direct questions about social distinctions. Why, for instance, if many generations ago the ancestor of a man was ennobled for great personal bravery, does one assume that his descendant, who might be a perfect coward, is still deserving of honor? What right have such men to behave with haughtiness and disdain toward men who might very well be their betters in all but birth? The answer, at this stage, is rather lame. Noblesse oblige, the bearers of great names must live up to them, otherwise they deserve to be held in contempt.[18] Capa-kaum is not satisfied and returns to the subject. He has noticed that men will make great sacrifices to acquire a patent of nobility. Once they have it, they are pleased to die so that they can display their new coats of arms on their coffins.[19] He receives no satisfactory answer to this question, but instead is invited to accompany his hosts on a tour of the countryside. They find lodgings with a peasant, but are given hardly anything to eat. Capa-kaum, whose appetite at least has not diminished since his arbitrary translation to the civilized world,

17. *Ibid.*, pp. 41–42.
18. *Ibid.*, p. 43.
19. *Ibid.*, pp. 59–60.

demands food. The peasant apologizes, saying he can hardly feed his own family, much less guests. How is this possible in the midst of a rich and fertile land? It seems that all the peasants of the district are as badly off. At best, they get a double yield on what they sow—this because they can maintain only one or at most two plowhorses, there is no pasturage for cattle, and thus there is not enough fertilizer. After the tithe, the payments due to the overlord, and the seed-corn have been put aside, there is very little left. Now if the unproductive upland field could be turned into a vineyard, or the lowland vineyard, which produces only vinegar, into a field, things might be better. But custom is king, no changes are permitted. And the payments in money due to the noble owner of the land are not only oppressive but come at the very worst time. What little fruit the peasants are able to raise as their only cash crop has to be dumped on the market in order to raise the cash. No wonder the peasants have to make do with a diet of bread, soup, and sauerkraut the year round.[20]

At this point Sonnenfels, stepping out of character for the moment, inserts an editorial comment addressed to those whom he judges responsible for these conditions. To the monarch he says that these miserable bondsmen make up the majority of his subjects. Only his strength stands between them and complete annihilation. Unless something is done for them soon, they will not even have enough strength left to beget children and thus replenish their numbers. The fields will be neglected and hunger will stalk the land. To the landowners he says: if the peasants go under, who will thereafter support them in the luxury in which they wallow? Will ruined serfs pay higher dues? Of course they can be driven from the land, but then, like Oriental despots, the nobles will rule over desert wastes. The merchants would also do well to look to the welfare of the peasants. In the absence of an agricultural surplus there can be no profits for

20. *Ibid.*, pp. 176ff.

them. Furthermore, it is notorious that there are no physicians to be found in the countryside. Indeed, who would pay them? Well, who better than the state, which had best look to the welfare of the majority of its subjects if it cares about its own survival.[21]

At this point Sonnenfels heard from the censors. For some time Cardinal Migazzi had been complaining about the tone of his journal toward the authority of the church in matters of conscience. Now that social and perhaps even political institutions were being subjected to criticism, these complaints were beginning to have additional weight. When there were actually some scattered peasant disorders, the authorities closed down the *Mann ohne Vorurteil*.[22] Sonnenfels, by putting to use all the influence he could muster, was able almost at once to get permission to resume publication, but only in exchange for his firm promise that henceforth he would leave the peasants strictly alone. He printed an indignant protest, denying that anything he might have written could possibly have been in any way responsible for the peasant revolts: as everyone knew, it was not the peasants but their oppressors who read his paper.[23] Nevertheless he capitulated, after publishing, as a last act of defiance, a gross attack on his defense of the peasants and his answer to this, in which he said that when the dogs wanted to run free, it was of no help to tell the huntsman to hold the leash all the more tightly, and that whereas the oldest and most honorable of the arts was agri-

21. *Ibid.*, pp. 196ff.

22. Zenker, *Wiener Journalistik*, p. 51. Migazzi was particularly angry about Sonnenfels' espousal of a proposal to diminish the number of public holidays, a proposal which, however, both Maria Theresa and Joseph backed with enthusiasm. See Kann, *Austrian Intellectual History*, p. 177. Van Swieten, who himself read and censored the periodical press and had passed the offending numbers, submitted his resignation, but Maria Theresa convinced him to remain. Müller, *Gerhard van Swieten*, p. 146.

23. Sonnenfels, *Gesammelte Schriften*, II, 226. It is not uninteresting that in one of his first university lectures in 1763 Sonnenfels had himself argued in favor of retaining the censorship, which was necessary in order to keep unrestrained opinion in check. See S. Brunner, *Die Mysterien der Aufklärung in Österreich: 1770–1800* (Mainz, 1869), p. 70.

culture, in Austria through prejudice and self-interest it had been reduced to the unhappiest of all occupations. So much the worse for society, for the state.[24]

Even though Sonnenfels was silenced, he had drawn attention to some very real problems and made some converts to his views. One of the members of the Urbarial Commission which was convened in 1767 to find a solution to the country's agricultural problems was Franz Anton von Blanc, who in the course of the commission's deliberations introduced a number of *vota* that seem to have been based in large part on Sonnenfels' opinions. Thus the patent of 1768 regulating and limiting the amount of service that could be required of the peasants, which was largely the result of Blanc's work, can indirectly be credited to Sonnenfels.[25]

From this point on Sonnenfels shifted his attack, first to the guilds, then back to his original target, the nobility.[26] The guilds were attacked for their membership restrictions. They prevent many qualified workers from working at their trades, says Sonnenfels. Now anyone not fortunate enough to possess a capital of his own can earn his living in only one of two ways: he can work, or he can steal. Whoever is prevented from doing the first must perforce resort to the second. In consequence the jails are filled. Men go through long and penurious apprenticeships, difficult and obligatory *Wanderjahre* far from their homes. Yet unless they are themselves the sons of master craftsmen, or succeed in marrying their daughters or widows, their chances of ever obtaining a master's certificate are as good as nil.[27] His study of the guilds leads him to make comparisons between them. It strikes him as peculiar that the most laborious trades are the worst paid and make the least provision for their practitioners,

24. Sonnenfels, *Gesammelte Schriften*, II, 227ff.
25. K. Grünberg, "Franz Anton von Blanc: Ein Sozialpolitiker der Theresianischen-Josephinischen Zeit," *Jahrbuch für Gesetzgebung, Verwaltung und Volkswirtschaft im Deutschen Reich*, n.F., XXXV (1911), 137–141.
26. Zenker, *Wiener Journalistik*, pp. 51–52.
27. Sonnenfels, *Gesammelte Schriften*, II, 237–239.

who are left weak and helpless in their old age.[28] Expanding on this theme, he raises the question of whether it is possible to establish by law a just equilibrium between the nature of work performed and its monetary reward. He observes that those who provide pleasures are paid out of all proportion in comparison to those who produce necessities. But he arrives at no real answer to the question.[29]

After a rather long interlude of publishing only harmless materials, Sonnenfels returned to the subject of the nobility. His approach was rather more careful the second time around. Ideally, he says, the number of the great should be reduced. Those who remained would be counted great for their merits alone. Yet nobility of birth by no means excludes nobility of actions. On the contrary, the one presupposes the other.[30] Again, no bourgeois anywhere dreams of begrudging the nobility the dignity of its bearing; only its pride is insufferable.[31] All attacks on the nobility can ultimately be distilled down to the proposition that birth alone bestows no special merit. This argument is to some extent mitigated by noblesse oblige, but in practice, unfortunately, it does not obligate all, or sufficiently. Thus the great advantages bestowed upon undeserving nobles must be regarded as a sort of injustice, a violation of the principle that only genuine merit should find its reward.[32] It is impossible to miss the increasingly tentative tone of these disquisitions. Every criticism is qualified, every attack halted well before its target is overrun. This was no doubt in part due to Sonnenfels' continuing difficulties with the censorship.

We are now in 1767. Sonnenfels had published a pamphlet which urged that measures be taken to reduce the population of Vienna and other large cities by forcibly resettling a percentage of their inhabitants in the countryside. This suggestion, in itself

28. *Ibid.*, p. 250.
29. *Ibid.*, pp. 256ff.
30. *Ibid.*, p. 323.
31. *Ibid.*, p. 348.
32. *Ibid.*, p. 352.

perfectly compatible with his concern over the plight of the rural areas, touched upon a sufficient number of powerful and vested interests so that a considerable storm now broke over his head. The result was that a preventive censorship was now imposed on all of his future writings. He appealed the decision to Maria Theresa and she decided that he should be permitted to continue writing so long as he himself imposed due moderation on the expression of his opinions.[33] He would certainly have been under the obligation of treading carefully from this point on. Still, a more fundamental change in Sonnenfels' whole outlook can be detected in this period. Instead of inveighing against any and all abuses, he seems to be convincing himself that change can only be brought about from the top, that only the state is powerful enough to cope with the pervasive abuses of society, that the only course open to a reasonable man is to support those in power and to hope that sooner or later he can convince them of the rightness of his views. He tries his hand at sycophancy: "A single word from the mouth of a Kaunitz, a smile from the lovely Princess Liechtenstein, are more to the poet in the way of reward than all the gold in the world."[34] Sonnenfels' attention is now increasingly concentrated on the person of the monarch. The later numbers of the *Mann ohne Vorurteil*, insofar as they are not filled with his increasingly inflexible opinions on the theater, resemble a *Fürstenspiegel*, flashed without much pretense of subtlety in the direction of Joseph.

In a labored parable the king of the ill-fated island realm of Ichnapuka comes to realize that he has been put on earth not in order to destroy the lives of his subjects but rather to enhance them. All wars are evil, and the wise ruler will flee thrice before he fights, because he realizes that the whole of the human race constitutes a single body, from which no limb may be cut without doing irreparable harm to the whole. The king in turn

33. Kann, *Austrian Intellectual History*, pp. 177–178.
34. Sonnenfels, *Gesammelte Schriften*, III, 113. Indeed, the third volume of the *Mann ohne Vorurteil* is dedicated to, of all people, Migazzi.

advises his subjects that so long as they devote their lives to work his rule will be a mild one, because "only the idle need rules, the worker has morals."[35]

There now comes one final foray onto sensitive ground. In an essay on education which is not only modeled upon Rousseau but explicitly calls attention to this fact, Sonnenfels dismisses what has so far been attempted as quite beside the point. Ideally, the state would assume full responsibility for the education of all children. Without regard to their social origin, their education would proceed with the same end in view for all. Unfortunately, so long as differences in men's estates and fortunes continue to exist, he does not see how this is to be implemented.[36]

The last political note in the *Mann ohne Vorurteil* is a warning to the monarch not to dispense the royal favor too freely. Not only is it counter-productive to put people into positions which their abilities do not entitle them to occupy, but subjects at all levels will attempt to make their careers on the strength of genuine merit as soon as they are convinced that they can expect no arbitrary favors.[37] There has been an unmistakable shift in emphasis: the purview is now that of a man seeking to advise his sovereign how best to cope with his difficult job. Social criticism has receded into the background.

Sonnenfels' weekly had many imitators, the work of lesser men who tried to share in his market without possessing his talent. These all disappeared after a few issues. Perhaps typical of them, and without doubt the most aptly named, was Ferdinand von Geusau's *Der hungrige Gelehrte*.[38]

In the same *annus mirabilis* which saw the grandeur and misery of the *Mann ohne Vorurteil*, Sonnenfels began the publication of his lecture notes for his course in political economy at the university. These were eventually gathered into three

35. Sonnenfels, *Gesammelte Schriften*, III, 226ff.

36. *Ibid.*, pp. 334ff.

37. *Ibid.*, pp. 525ff., 544.

38. Others were the *Verbesserer, Schwatzer, Aufseher, Zuschauer, Freund der Tugend, Lehrling, Einsiedler,* and *Freunde*. See Zenker, *Wiener Journalistik*, p. 52.

volumes under the title *Grundsätze der Polizey, Handlung und Finanzwirtschaft.*[39] Although the first two volumes are introduced by quotations from Rousseau, the tone of the work is throughout one of careful reserve. Apparently Sonnenfels, who was willing, if only briefly, to play the role of fiery journalist, in his academic function did not pursue his enthusiasms with equal vigor. In general, his political views published in the *Grundsätze* are much less adventurous than those of the *Mann ohne Vorurteil,* while his opinions on social and economic questions, although more carefully phrased, tend to be very similar.

Aristocracy is commented upon only in its historical context, as a possible alternative form of government to monarchy and democracy. With respect to the latter, a warning is given about allowing undue influence to the mob, which, having nothing to lose, will take great risks to attain its ends.[40] In times of social tension it is essential to exercise a preventive state censorship as well as the normally existing one, and it is to the general advantage of the state to abolish newspapers altogether.[41] Freedoms exist only insofar as the laws do not abrogate them.[42] The censorship is necessary in order to prevent the dissemination of erroneous, aggravating, and dangerous opinions. It must be extended not merely to books, but to plays, lectures, newspapers, prints, and any other materials intended for the general public. But the censors must do their work with great good sense. Because just as too great a liberty of the press is the mother of unbelief, civil disorders, and scandalous laxity of morals, an exaggerated severity is deleterious to the development of the sciences.[43]

The sections dealing with the causes of rural poverty, al-

39. J. v. Sonnenfels, *Grundsätze der Polizey, Handlung und Finanzwirtschaft* (3 vols., Vienna, 1765–67). I have used the third edition of 1770, but differences are minimal.

40. *Ibid.,* I, 22–23.

41. *Ibid.,* pp. 92–93.

42. *Ibid.,* p. 103. Is Sonnenfels the originator of the old joke that in Germany everything that is not specifically allowed is forbidden?

43. *Ibid.,* pp. 141–150.

though without the impassioned rhetoric of the *Mann ohne Vorurteil,* convey essentially the same message: the administrator must realize that a portion of the peasantry is apt to give way to despair at any given moment because it is continually being threatened with utter ruin. The main causes for this, apart from the uncertainty of nature's bounty, are the inordinately large payments that have to be made to the landlord, the continual hunts that the latter engages in to the great detriment of the peasant, and the excessive number of religious holidays.[44] Particularly damaging to the economy are the still-persisting labor obligations, the so-called *Robot,* which many of the peasants are required to perform for their lords. It would be preferable by far to commute these into money payments at a rate which the peasants can afford.[45]

Finally, Sonnenfels introduces a theme which he had not touched on in his journalism, perhaps because he believed it to be too incendiary to be discussed by the nonacademic public. In measured terms, but without compromise, he condemns the use of torture to determine the guilt or innocence of an accused. Apart from the questionable legality of applying, while there is still a presumption of innocence, something possibly more painful than any eventual punishment that might result if guilt were established, the method is not even reliable. The inexperienced and weak will confess to any crime with which they are charged at the mere sight of the instruments of torture, while the tough and already brutalized criminal will be acquitted in spite of his certain guilt.[46]

In addition, the death penalty should also be abolished. Its main fault is its ineffectiveness as a deterrent: those who commit capital crimes are perfectly aware that it awaits them if they are caught, but their existences are at any rate so miserable that they are indifferent to death. A far greater evil, in their view, is to be

44. *Ibid.,* II, 57–58.
45. *Ibid.,* pp. 115–117.
46. *Ibid.,* I, 108–111.

forced to perform hard and regular work. Therefore, let capital punishment be replaced by life imprisonment at hard labor. This would be a really effective deterrent.[47]

Because of his continuing efforts on behalf of these causes, Sonnenfels, who was otherwise to become indistinguishable from the run-of-the-mill smug public official of a more or less enlightened absolutism, has retained a reputation as a liberal. The Censorship Commission was not unaware of his opinions on these subjects and made representations directly to Maria Theresa. In 1769, after the promulgation of the reformed code of criminal law, the *Nemesis Theresiana*, Sonnenfels complained that it retained all the old barbarous punishments. Count Rudolph Chotek, the court chancellor, now asked the Empress to command him to lecture only in accordance with the existing structure of law, but she decided that he should be permitted to continue to teach as his principles bade him to do. Three years later, however, the commission, this time without first making an inquiry at the top, issued an order forbidding Sonnenfels to speak in public about torture. He at once appealed this directive to the Empress, who decided that while he had done nothing remiss in speaking his mind on the subject, and while none of his writings were to be withdrawn, he was to say nothing further. On this peculiar and characteristically Austrian compromise the matter rested for some years. Then, in 1775, the whole question was discussed at length at a number of meetings of the Government of Lower Austria. Sonnenfels testified before it repeatedly, and suddenly the whole of his testimony, rehearsing all the old arguments, appeared for sale in the form of a pamphlet.[48] Called to order by the Censorship Commission, he answered that none of this was of his making. He had shown the transcript of his testimony to some friends, and they must have decided on their own initiative to print it. The story was hardly convincing,

47. *Ibid.*, pp. 452–455.
48. J. v. Sonnenfels, *Über die Abschaffung der Folter* (Vienna, 1775).

but the damage was done. The debate had now become an exceedingly public one.[49]

The precise sequence of the events that followed is not clear. There is a story that Sonnenfels, in a private audience with Maria Theresa, fell on his knees in a moment charged with emotion and won her over. This tale is almost certainly apocryphal. It is rather more probable that Joseph, finally convinced by Sonnenfels' arguments, swayed his mother. At any rate, in 1776 preliminary torture was abolished. It was no insignificant victory for an ex-Jew to have won in Theresan Austria.[50]

What sort of man was it, then, who alternately railed at and flattered the nobility, and who insisted upon the necessity of retaining the very censorship which was constantly engaged in suppressing his own work? Even if one makes every allowance for the fact that he could sail only so close to the wind, these contradictions cannot readily be explained away as the result of mere tactical necessity. It has been suggested that "he thought as an absolutist and felt as a democrat" and that, being a rational man, he chose to take the part of the still extremely viable autocracy. Thus, rather than being a pioneer of democracy, he was the last of the Cameralists.[51] As far as it goes, there is much to be said for this argument. But it fails to explain why Sonnenfels should have, over a period of many years, persisted in an elaborate campaign to abolish torture and capital punishment when it was quite clear that the whole weight of the establishment was arrayed against him.

He has also been dismissed as a loquacious imitator of the French enlightenment whose work was not only entirely de-

49. Müller, *Josef von Sonnenfels*, pp. 129–138; Deutsch, "Joseph von Sonnenfels," p. 73; Kann, *Austrian Intellectual History*, pp. 184–186.

50. Kann, *Austrian Intellectual History*, p. 184. Torture was retained in Hungary, whose government apparently could not do without it, and also as an aggravation of punishment in the case of convicted criminals whose offenses were judged to be particularly heinous. The death penalty, although in theory retained, was abolished de facto after Joseph's accession as sole ruler in 1780.

51. G. P. Gooch, *Germany and the French Revolution* (London, 1920), p. 22.

rivative, but made no attempt whatever to find points of repair in the local environment. As his arguments were wholly abstract, so were his conclusions. He finished by worshiping the state in the naively idealized form of enlightened monarchy.[52] Apart from the fact that these strictures evidently were formed without reference to the *Mann ohne Vorurteil*, they are also wide of the mark in a broader, conceptual sense. Within the German-speaking context, Sonnenfels was anything but a late comer re-peating shopworn platitudes long ago emptied of their content. Instead, he was a genuine pioneer. Even in the Protestant north, it was not until 1759 that Friedrich Karl Moser in *Der Herr und der Diener* dared to use the insolent tone toward constituted authority which Sonnenfels habitually resorted to in 1765–66. Sonnenfels may have been a spiritual Cameralist; certainly in later life he surrounded himself with an impenetrable wall of pendantry and pomposity. Joseph, who wittingly or not had derived a surprising number of his favorite ideas from Sonnen-fels' works, couldn't stand him, and after Maria Theresa's death in 1780 he found himself both isolated and excluded from the avenues of power. His odes to the monarch had to be delivered from the lectern rather than in the palace. There was something inherently ridiculous in this position and so it is no wonder that Sonnenfels became an object of ridicule. But no man's youth should be judged by his old age. The Sonnenfels of the *Mann ohne Vorurteil*, the tireless campaigner for the abolition of tor-ture, was for a time one of the great German liberals. On this point I disagree, in part, with a recent account which attempts to explain the contradictions within Sonnenfels by maintaining that he must be viewed within the context of enlightened ab-solutism and should not be regarded as part of a "pre-liberal movement." In addition, Sonnenfels and others of a like mind

52. Magris, *Habsburgischer Mythos*, p. 30. Magris bases these opinions largely on Sonnenfels' *Über die Liebe des Vaterlandes*, which Goethe at the time re-jected as too general and abstract to promote genuine feelings of patriotism in real persons. Goethe's review appeared in the *Frankfurter gelehrten Anzeiger* for 1771. See Nagl, Zeidler, and Castle, *Literaturgeschichte*, II, 256.

"used the oppressive methods of the system to gain their objectives instead of fighting these methods and thereby risking failure."[53] This explains only one facet of his behavior. I am rather inclined to believe that both Sonnenfels in 1765–66 and many of his successors and imitators offered advice so radical that had it been taken the system would not have been able to absorb it. These men were no republicans, but the changes they wished to bring about in the monarchy were such as to introduce into it most of the republican qualities they evidently admired. Sonnenfels' abandonment of the liberal position for one that has been aptly called "reform conservatism"[54] was most probably the result of sober calculation: he had read the signs, he saw that the future belonged to Joseph, and he hoped to work through him. It was not an unreasonable miscalculation. But even though he abandoned it, the position he had previously occupied remains a liberal one.

53. Kann, *Austrian Intellectual History*, p. 197.
54. K. Epstein, *The Genesis of German Conservatism* (Princeton, 1966), p. 412.

3
Church, Censorship, and Intelligentsia

In 1759 the Jesuits were expelled from Portugal, in 1763 from France, in 1767 from Spain and Naples. Thereafter the Bourbon courts began to exert very considerable pressure on Rome to dissolve the Society. Clement XIV, who donned the papal tiara in 1769, let it be known that he would agree to such a step if all the Catholic monarchs of Europe would support him in it. All the others having preceded her, the issue was now squarely up to Maria Theresa. For four years the Empress, who was genuinely fond of the Society, and who had since the death of her husband rather exceeded the norms of piety expected of even a widow, resisted all entreaties. At last, convinced that to do otherwise would be to act in a sense contrary to the interests of the state, she gave way. In July, 1773, the papal proclamation *Dominus ac Redemptor noster* dissolved the Society. In September it was read from all pulpits in Austria.[1]

The property of the Jesuits was confiscated. Their archives were sold as scrap paper and fetched the sum of sixty-one florins. The membership had the option of leaving the country or the Society. In Austria, where they had played such an influential role in the political and intellectual life of the country, their disappearance was bound to have considerable effect. In actual fact

1. Tomek, *Kirchengeschichte*, III, pp. 234–239.

this effect was considerably less than had been predicted. In politics their influence had long been on the wane, and in intellectual life they had not been nearly as influential as they had supposed. The disappearance of the Society did not, as its spokesmen had been predicting, bring about a dark age of ignorance. Quite the contrary: a surprising number of ex-Jesuits chose to remain in Austria, willing to grasp whatever opportunities might present themselves to live by their wits. Released from the constraints under which they had formerly lived, they were now able to put their traditionally good educations to a use for which they had never been intended. Many ex-Jesuits, like Franz Xaver Alois Mayer, who became rector of the University of Graz, or Count Hohenwart, tutor to Leopold II, were able to serve the new order in the same capacities that they had occupied in the old.[2] Many more, less fortunate, were hard put to find careers commensurate with their education and former station in life. The career of literatus could not fail to attract them if it were at all possible to make a living at it.[3]

So long as Maria Theresa lived, the market for literary talent can best be described as weak to variable. The Empress, as she settled into old age, did not depart noticeably from the prejudices of her youth. If anything, she was more convinced than formerly that one of her foremost responsibilities to God was to protect her subjects from the dissemination of insidious and corrupting opinions. She decreed that no chair of English literature should ever be established in a university within her dominions, as practically the whole literary corpus of that language was no better than a deliberate attack on religion and morality.[4] And although

2. Krones, *Karl-Franzens Universität*, p. 456.

3. All members of the Society who remained in Austria were given the sum of 100 florins to purchase a suit of secular dress, but thereafter those who found no regular employment had to make do on a monthly pension of 16 florins, not a munificent sum. See L. v. Pastor, *The History of the Popes from the Close of the Middle Ages*, trans. E. F. Peeler (40 vols., London, 1891–1953), XXXVIII, 341–347.

4. Müller, "Absolutismus," p. 23.

it was widely known that she was an avid reader of the weekly published in Göttingen by August Ludwig Schlötzer, sometimes even interjecting into a meeting with her ministers the question "what would Schlötzer say about this?," she was unwilling to grant anyone the same freedoms within her dominions; Sonnenfels was to remain unique in having enjoyed that privilege.[5] The presidency of the Censorship Commission had, after Koch's undistinguished tenure, been taken over by Count Leopold Clary. It was said of him that, whereas under van Swieten twenty good books out of a hundred had been banned, now the ratio was reversed.[6] This seemed to suit Maria Theresa, and Joseph chose to argue with his mother on other and more immediate issues.

One could, however, write for the theater, where sheer productivity could secure a reasonable living for an enterprising author. And in spite of Hägelin's unremitting watchfulness, it was very occasionally possible to smuggle some political or religious opinions into a play. One such attempt was Ferdinand Eberl's *Das listige Stubenmädchen*, now lost, which in one scene portrayed a lawyer making up an expense account for a journey from which he had just returned and including twelve ducats for the purpose of bribing his confessor to grant him absolution for his transgressions. To be sure, the play was closed down and the management fined.[7]

A much more serious thinker was the dramatist Paul Weidmann. Born in Vienna in 1746, he was sent to school with the Jesuits, attended the university, and in 1767 entered upon government service, accepting a position as a clerk in the encoding

---

5. Gooch, *Germany and the French Revolution*, p. 21. Göttingen was on Hanoverian territory and Hanover was united with England in a personal union. Even so, Schlötzer was allowed to write what he pleased only on condition that he refrain from concerning himself with local affairs. On the one occasion on which he violated this rule he was put in jail.

6. Sashegyi, *Zensur und Geistesfreiheit*, p. 16.

7. O. Rommel, *Die Alt-Wiener Volkskomödie* (Vienna, 1952), p. 451.

department. Being both a pupil of the Jesuits and a poet-bureaucrat, he deserves our closer scrutiny. His job must not have taken up all of his time and energy, as in 1771 he began writing plays and over the next ten years turned out, on the average, something over five a year. He is best known for his *Johann Faust*, written and produced in 1775 and thus contemporaneous with Goethe's rather better-known play on the same subject. Weidmann's *Faust*, insofar as it is remembered at all, is noted for having introduced theodicy as a central theme into the old story, and because (as was not the case with Goethe, who needed a second part to get the job done) his protagonist is saved in the last act.[8] Apart from this, the play really does not seem to be concerned very directly with politics, although the censors in Munich banned it, more apparently on general principles than for any specific transgression.[9] An earlier play of Weidmann's, however, was considerably less innocuous.

In 1773 the Burgtheater played Weidmann's *Die Folter, oder der menschliche Richter*, which was nothing less than a dramatization of Sonnenfels' notorious campaign to abolish torture, and this at a time when Sonnenfels himself was under orders not to speak in public on the subject. The play portrays the misadventures of a young man mistakenly accused of a crime, who confesses his guilt under torture and is about to be executed, when at the very last moment his innocence is established. To rather gild the lily, the judge who had pronounced sentence of death on him discovers that he is his long-lost son. Thereupon he resigns his charge and in a curtain speech directed unmistakably at the imperial box asks God to teach monarchs to love mankind

8. P. Weidmann, *Johann Faust* (Prague, 1775). On Weidmann see Wurzbach, *Biographisches Lexicon*, LIII, 272–273; Mühlher, "Literatur der Aufklärung," p. 292; O. Rommel, "Rationalistische Dämonie: Die Geister-Romane des ausgehenden 18. Jahrhunderts," *D.V.L.G.*, XVII (1939), 217; R. Payer v. Thurn, "Paul Weidmann, der Wiener Faust-Dichter des 18. Jahrhunderts," *J.G.G.*, XIII (1903), 1–74; and K. Adel's introduction to a reprinting of *Johann Faust* (Vienna, 1964).

9. R. Payer v. Thurn's appendix to a reprinting of *Johann Faust* (Vienna, 1911), pp. 19–22.

and to weigh blood with jeweler's scales, lest one day they be asked to repay Him with theirs.[10] While hardly a great play, *Die Folter* is a bold venture onto ground hitherto not accessible to dramatic literature. It is difficult to comprehend how it ever got past the censors.

In the same year in which he produced his *Faust*, Weidmann tried his hand for the first time at historical drama, an art form which, if successfully mastered, traditionally bestowed a reputation of a higher order on its practitioners than that enjoyed by scribblers of merely occasional pieces. His efforts were poorly constructed and in consequence were badly received by the critics. But in one of them, *Das befreyte Wien*, which dealt with conditions in the city after the lifting of the Turkish siege, he puts into the mouth of Count Rüdiger von Starhemberg some observations about the unequal rewards that the monarch bestows upon the different estates: in the aftermath of the victory, the aristocracy has been surfeited with new titles and dignities; the humble man is asked to risk his life for little or nothing. Still, he does so willingly. At the very least, the disproportionate rewards they receive should impose upon noblemen a higher sense of their responsibilities.[11]

In 1778 Weidmann wrote a comedy with unmistakable political connotations, *Der Misbrauch der Gewalt*. He drew upon both his literary and bureaucratic experience to produce the redoubtable but ridiculous figure of Count Diestelthal. Not blessed unduly with ability, this gentleman makes up for that lack by running the government office which he heads with a mixture of injustice, harshness, and parsimony. He rejects all pleas from his subordinates for higher pay with indignant declarations to the effect that officials have absolutely no need to eat meat in order to do their jobs acceptably. He rails against intellectual as well as physical hunger. People should be forcibly

10. Adel, intro., *Faust*, p. 8; Payer v. Thurn, "Paul Weidmann," pp. 38–41.
11. Adel, intro., *Faust*, p. 8; Payer v. Thurn, "Paul Weidmann," p. 33.

prevented from partaking of the poisons that even the best books contain. He spends his days in engaging in shady financial speculations, and when one of his senior officials objects, he has him thrown into jail. The mounted messenger of the king arrives in the nick of time in the guise of a reform-minded count and all ends well, but the attack on the misdeeds of high officialdom is not to be missed. The play ran for one performance and the next day was closed down with the injunction that it should never be performed again.[12] Still, it had passed the censorship initially, and nothing was done to Weidmann in the aftermath. His partial immunity, which extended also to his career as an official, in which he indulged himself all his life in the dangerous pleasure of denouncing his superiors, was probably the direct result of another comedy, produced in 1776, *Der Bettelstudent*. This thin farce at once became Maria Theresa's favorite play. On one occasion she said that she hoped to see it a hundred times before being forced once again to sit through Lessing's *Emilia Galotti*.[13] This partiality was well known, and so long as the Empress lived, did Weidmann no harm.

After Maria Theresa's death Weidmann's star waned rapidly. The public grew tired of his plays, and Joseph, whom he bombarded with long proposals for reforming various branches of the state service, resisted all his advances. On one occasion he told him, "your writings contain much truth, but I don't care for your style."[14] Weidmann tried repeatedly to make a place for himself as a spokesman for Josephinian absolutism, but without success. His hour had come and gone. He was to re-emerge from

12. P. Weidmann, *Der Misbrauch der Gewalt* (Vienna, 1778); Payer v. Thurn, app., *Faust*, pp. 41–42.

13. Payer v. Thurn, app., *Faust*, p. 50. As *Emilia Galotti*, at least by indirection, attacks the social irresponsibility of court culture, Maria Theresa's professing to have grown tired of the play may have been the result of an instinctive recognition that her world was under attack. See Bruggemann, "Der Kampf," p. 100.

14. R. Payer v. Thurn, "Eine politische Denkschrift Paul Weidmann's," *J.G.G.*, XVI (1906), 281.

the murky half-light of reluctantly performed official duties only briefly, and not until after the Emperor's death.[15]

The strange career of Weidmann apart, the only field which offered at least a partial opportunity for the expression of hetero-dox opinions in Maria Theresa's last years was, paradoxically, ecclesiastical history. Here, in spite of the Empress' piety, it was possible to take the side of royal prerogative and, sheltering be-hind that shield, let loose a multiple attack on the church. Such works were sure to find immediate approval in the eyes of Prince Kaunitz, who could on occasion even be moved to extend his patronage to their authors. If necessary, he was always willing to mobilize Joseph's support on behalf of a writer who had tran-scended the limits of the acceptable. And so long as the debate remained within the confines of the academic world, and could be represented as merely a logical extension of the views of Justi and Martini, there was unlikely to be any undue interference on the part of the authorities. It is in this context that the career of men such as Joseph Valentin Eybel should be understood.

Eybel, born in Vienna in 1741, was educated by the Jesuits, took his vows, and joined the Society, but in 1765 left it for Graz, where for a time he occupied a minor clerical post. When he returned to Vienna, it was to take up the study of law at the uni-versity. He was one of Riegger's best students, and upon his grad-uation his career was regarded as so promising that when Riegger retired in 1773, Eybel was appointed as his successor. He soon came into conflict with Cardinal Migazzi by speaking out in fa-vor of the opinions of a Father Dionysius Kaltner, who main-tained that the church had no right to put obstacles in the way of those whom social considerations obliged to marry.[16] Eventu-ally this stand earned him a reprimand from Maria Theresa. In

---

15. The last act in Weidmann's career as a social critic was a defense of Joseph's toleration policies, in the play *Stephan Fädinger*, performed in 1781.

16. Wurzbach, *Biographisches Lexicon*, IV, 118; Wolfsgruber, *C. A. K. Migaz-zi*, p. 348.

1777 he published an *Introduction to Canon Law*, whose theme was that in all areas where religion touched upon vital concerns of the state it was subject to the authority of the monarch.[17] In spite of this, Maria Theresa regarded him as unreliable in theological questions, and in 1779 she backed an intrigue of Migazzi's which resulted in Eybel's dismissal from his post at the University of Vienna.[18] Joseph complained to his brother Leopold about the inconsequential intrigues that were afoot, the influence of petty and vindictive men who pushed the Empress into making decisions in an area that she understood but dimly, and the waste of money that all this entailed, but did nothing.[19] Eybel wound up with a distinctly inferior position in the Government of Upper Austria in Linz. Some years later he would emerge from this obscurity briefly with a rather sad and unsuccessful attempt to bring himself to Joseph's attention.[20]

A somewhat similar but eminently more successful career was that of Franz Stephan Rautenstrauch. Abbot of the great Benedictine double monastery at Braunau-Břevnov in Bohemia, Rautenstrauch had high connections in Vienna. His reputation as a progressive monk brought him to the attention of a small but influential circle known as *Die Grossen in Wien*. This discussion group initially encompassed only van Swieten, Martini, Bishop Stock, and Müller, the Empress' confessor. They met weekly to consider how best the church might be reformed and what guidelines ought to govern its relations with the state. Later, Rautenstrauch and Baron Franz Karl Kressel, who afterward was to become one of the leading instruments of Josephinian church reform, were admitted to the circle. The whole tenor of these meetings was strongly Jansenist-Febronian. In 1773, Stock having died, Rautenstrauch's friends used their influence to secure

17. Lhotsky, *Historiographie*, p. 124.
18. Wolfsgruber, *C. A. K. Migazzi*, p. 384.
19. Arneth, *Maria Theresia und Joseph*, III, 235–236.
20. Wolfsgruber, *C. A. K. Migazzi*, pp. 385–386.

for him one of the late Bishop's dignities, the directorship of Austrian theological studies. As his appointment coincided with the disorder and confusion that followed upon the expulsion of the Jesuits, he now found that he disposed over not inconsiderable powers of innovation. In 1774 he produced a plan of studies which departed almost entirely from the Jesuitical practice of emphasizing Scholastic philosophy, and instead concentrated on the teaching of pastoral theology. At about this time he was also appointed to the Censorship Commission. In conjunction with his views on educational reform, he now developed a Jansenist-inspired doctrine on the supremacy of the secular over the religious sphere. Therefrom he derived the right of monarchs to tolerate minority religions in their dominions.[21]

This, however, was the extent of Rautenstrauch's willingness to encompass radical change. By temperament he was essentially a conservative; he despised Sonnenfels as a reckless innovator. Still, his publications as well as the academic reforms which he introduced later on greatly facilitated the task of those willing to subject the church to a more searching scrutiny than he was.

It is now necessary to return to the topic of censorship. We have seen how, having been somewhat relaxed, it nevertheless continued to exercise a stringent if rather sporadic control over Austria's literary output. In addition, foreign books, although most of them would ultimately be passed, were held up for at least three months at the frontiers, apparently on the principle that if they contained really outrageous material, the Censorship Commission should be given the opportunity to hear about it elsewhere, without having to trouble itself to turn it up by its own efforts. After the unfortunate experience of the *Mann ohne Vorurteil*, the periodical press was subjected to a particularly close scrutiny. The only newspaper to appear with any regularity or frequency, the *Wiener Zeitung*, was allowed only to publish

21. *Ibid.*, p. 352; Tomek, *Kirchengeschichte*, III, 617; Winter, *Der Josephinismus*, pp. 34, 74–77.

such news of the internal affairs of the monarchy as was supplied to it by the various ministries.[22]

This, then, was the situation which obtained when, on November 29, 1780, Maria Theresa died. Contrary to what is generally assumed, Joseph did not at once engage in a headlong rush to abolish all of his mother's system of government. But in the matter of censorship, which he had long regarded as a blot on the national honor, insofar as its rigorous enforcement by the customs convinced foreign travelers that his dominions were both backward and obscurantist, he did think that some haste was not undue. The question was submitted to the *Staatsrat*, and Kaunitz was given the task of steering a more liberal law through that body. He argued that the exaggerated severity of the censorship had, without achieving the end of preventing really perfidious literature from circulating, greatly hampered the most desirable goal of national enlightenment and the orderly progress of science. He was ably supported in this cause by Baron Tobias von Gebler, a rising star in the Josephinian constellation. The new law which the *Staatsrat* recommended, and which was announced on March 11, 1781, was far from a total lifting of the censorship. It continued the prohibition of works offensive to religion, morals, and the welfare of the state. In addition, it forbade superstitious and mystical rantings about the nature of God, a useful weapon to have in hand against the conservative opponents of Joseph's ecclesiastical policies who were much given to that sort of speculation.[23] The new law, if clarity is taken as the chief criterion of great legislation, is no masterpiece. Its language is murky, and by itself it might not have brought about much in the way of change. The crux of the matter, however,

22. Zenker, *Wiener Journalistik*, p. 66; Goldfriedrich, *Deutschen Buchhandels*, p. 347.

23. Sashegyi, *Zensur und Geistesfreiheit*, pp. 21–28; P. v. Mitrofanov, *Joseph II.: Seine politische und kulturelle Tatigkeit*, trans V. v. Demelic (2 vols., Vienna and Leipzig, 1910), II, 826–829. The text of the law given in Gnau (*Die Zensur*, pp. 255–267) is incomplete.

must be sought in its interpretation and enforcement, and here Joseph, in part because he could never pass up the chance to make small economies, in part as a matter of policy, brought about a very considerable relaxation of the censorship.

The new president of the Censorship Commission, Count Rudolph Chotek, although in many ways a traditionalist, was a cultured and in some ways enlightened man and hardly the sort of unbending fanatic it would have taken to oppose both Joseph and Kaunitz. In 1782, as part of an attempt to save money, the Censorship Commission was abolished and its work was turned over to the Educational Commission, at whose head Gott-fried van Swieten, the son of Gerhard, was placed. His views on religion were as advanced as those of his father had been, and he by far surpassed him in his admiration for the general ideals of the enlightenment. He employed as his chief censors the poet Alois Blumauer for belles lettres; a Father Rosalino, rather a nonentity, for theology; Baron Alois Locella, a liberal-minded admirer of the enlightenment, for political literature; and added periodical literature to Hägelin's responsibility for the theater. In sum, there were now two undoubted liberals, one unknown quantity (Rosalino), and one conservative who administered the censorship. It emerged before long that these men would also have to do nearly all the work themselves. In 1784, on the Emperor's orders, the total number of censors was reduced to nine, and somewhat later even further to six. Joseph reasoned that during the previous year some 2,800 works had been submitted to the censorship, and that one censor could easily cope with 300 a year. And one supposes that having survived this regimen for a time, he could step up his production to 500.[24]

Martini suggested to the Emperor that one could save even more money by turning responsibility for the censorship back to the university: the professors would not have to be paid any-thing at all, as it was in any case their duty to read everything

24. Mitrofanov, *Joseph II*, II, 795; Sashegyi, *Zensur und Geistesfreiheit*, pp. 40–52.

that was printed in their fields. But Joseph, who had little trust in the accomplishments of higher learning, forbore to take advantage of this ultimate economy. On the whole, there can be no question but that the conditions for what would be, at least for a time, a de facto immunity from censorship had been created. This was reinforced by the appointment of Joseph von Retzer, a Mason and Voltaire enthusiast, as censor for foreign publications.[25]

In conjunction with the loosening of the censorship, Joseph ordered a complete revision of the *Catalogum librorum prohibitorum*. Whole categories of works were now removed from it, including those that had been banned for merely casting doubts on the absolute nature of temporal or religious government. Van Swieten, backed always by Kaunitz, cut to the bone. The result was that whereas under Maria Theresa the *Catalogum* had, in its edition of 1774, encompassed a stately 4,476 titles, the new edition was reduced to 900. Those books still to be banned were divided into four categories: pornographic literature, works likely to abet superstition, books attacking the Christian religion *ex professo*, and books judged to be politically dangerous. The last category contained, among others, most of Hume's writings, some of Voltaire's *Tales*, Goethe's *Werther*, and Klopstock's *Ode to Joseph*, to which the Emperor had taken a violent dislike. There was a fifth category of works deemed to be especially corrupting, books which were to be kept out of the country at all costs. Making up this last circle were the works of Malebranche, Helvétius, Mirabeau, and Lessing's *Von dem Zwecke Jesu und seiner Jünger*. Nevertheless, the overall reduction in forbidden titles was impressive.[26]

The immediate fruits of this relaxation were, as was only to be expected, notable more for their profusion than for their quality. A seemingly endless number of pamphlets, the so-called *Broschürenflut*, swept over the land. Whoever had learned to

25. Sashegyi, *Zensur und Geistesfreiheit*, p. 50.
26. *Ibid.*, pp. 110–115.

write now took pen in hand, and the printers could hardly keep up. The *Hofkanzlei* complained in October, 1781, thus no more than seven months after the introduction of the new law, that several hundred pamphlets had already appeared in Vienna, out of which number, with the utmost forbearance, it was possible to find some literary merit in perhaps half a dozen. In an attempt to stem the flood, the publication of anonymous pamphlets was forbidden, but to no avail.[27] The scribblers were not to be deterred and continued to publish, either under their own names or under borrowed ones. No subject was too trivial for literary exploitation, and as a successful pamphlet was at once imitated, there would be dozens of them on a given theme until the public lost interest and began to read about something else. One such cluster of pamphlets was devoted to the subject of housemaids. Although an occasional attempt was made to dip into the social significance attendant upon the many degradations of this undoubtedly much-abused class, the real concern of the pamphleteers visibly lay elsewhere. The originator of this particular genre, Johann Rautenstrauch (not to be confused with the abbot of that name), did not mince words: hardly a young man walks the streets of Vienna who has not already been seduced by the family maid; hardly an older man who does not avail himself of the same opportunities. Why are these girls so successful in attracting men? Because of the attractive dirndls that they wear, allowing a generous and for the most part irresistible view of their bosoms.[28] Evidently Rautenstrauch had found a way of not running afoul of the stringent regulations against pornography by assuming a self-righteous and morally indignant tone and by cloaking his salacious points in just enough of a mantle of social significance. Whether or not his analysis of the role of housemaids in Austrian life was accurate remains a moot point, but one fact speaks in his favor: shortly after the appearance of his mono-

27. *Ibid.*, pp. 103–105; Nagl, Zeidler, and Castle, *Literaturgeschichte*, II, 286–290.
28. Gugitz, "Stubenmädchenliteratur," pp. 140–144.

graph, the Viennese ladies of the night began making their rounds dressed as housemaids.

Most of the pamphlets, however, were not even titillating: they were merely dull trash. Yet the public bought them up, read them avidly in the coffee houses (which soon found that they had to put in a stock of the latest publications if they wished to retain their customers), and discussed them heatedly. The Kaffee zum Kramer on the Graben was a favorite gathering place of the literary public. So many of the thriftier Viennese were availing themselves of the opportunity to read for the price of their afternoon refreshment that in self-defense Trattner opened a reading room, where for the modest membership fee of two florins a month one could peruse all the publications of his house.[29] A *Lesewut*, a veritable rage to read, took hold of Vienna. The suspicion that the readers were as undemanding as the writers were unsophisticated is hard to put down. Nevertheless, this literary explosion created enough of a stir in erudite circles so that, toward the end of 1781, no lesser figure than the Berlin publisher and bookseller Friedrich Nicolai, editor of the influential *Allgemeine Deutsche Bibliothek*, the would-be pope of German letters, decided to look the situation over for himself. Nicolai had for some time stood his ground on the argument that Austria's political alliance with France was the final proof, if proof were still needed, of her cultural depravity. For this Prussian nationalist to come to Vienna at all was a major concession. His visit did not begin auspiciously. At the border the customs officers insisted on examining his luggage for forbidden books. He protested that in accordance with the most recent legislation foreigners were exempt from such searches, but was told no such instructions had ever reached that particular crossing point. As a result, some of his books were taken away from him. He was not in the best of moods when he reached Vienna, and his temper hardly improved when he found that his reputation had apparently not preceded

---

29. E. Zellwerker, *Das Urbild des Sarastro: Ignaz von Born* (Vienna, 1953), p. 52.

him. He was not invited to the right parties, or seated high enough along the table at the ones he was invited to.[30]

Nicolai did get an invitation to the house of his long-time correspondent, Baron Gebler. The latter, who had literary ambitions of his own, had made a practice of sending his efforts to Nicolai for comment and advice and made a point of entertaining him now that he was in Vienna. The occasion, however, was spoiled. Since his arrival Nicolai had been followed everywhere by a mysterious cloaked figure, a man who, it was alleged by those whom Nicolai asked, was an ex-Jesuit, now a spy in the employ of the Archbishop. When his invitation to Gebler's table was brought by one of the Baron's servants, this man approached Nicolai directly and demanded that he be invited as well. When, somewhat intimidated, Nicolai approached his prospective host with this proposal, Gebler refused on the ground that the party would be made up of the most enlightened men in Vienna, the conversation would no doubt be unrestrained, and the presence of this man would constitute a dampening effect. In spite of this the gloomy ex-Jesuit appeared uninvited in the middle of dinner, and to Nicolai's astonishment, Gebler, although obviously out of sorts, did not dare turn him out.[31]

Nicolai left Austria in a foul mood and did not wait long to take his revenge in the form of a blanket denunciation of Austrian letters: the ceaseless scribbling that had seized the Austrians at the death of Maria Theresa simply would not stop; nothing revealed the cultural backwardness of that country more mercilessly than the passive acceptance of such masses of junk by the reading public. In spite of this, he had resolved to report on Viennese literature in the pages of the *Allgemeine Deutsche*

30. Sashegyi, *Zensur und Geistesfreiheit*, p. 79; Nagl, Zeidler, and Castle, *Literaturgeschichte*, II, 17–19; Nadler, *Literaturgeschichte*, p. 191.

31. R. M. Werner, *Aus dem Josephinischem Wien* (Berlin, 1888), pp. 4–12, 153. Nicolai's social difficulties in Vienna annoyed him to the point where he avenged himself at every opportunity. He disparaged the intellectual climate of Austria in a journal of his trip that he published shortly afterward, not even stopping short of ridiculing a *Wunderkind* to whom he had been introduced, little Karoline Greiner, who was to become the famous diarist Karoline Pichler.

Bibliothek in order that the Austrian public might be instructed to differentiate between what was good and what was bad. Failing that, there was no hope for it at all.[32] Unfortunately, what has been remembered by posterity is Nicolai's general condemnation of Austrian letters, and not the fact that, his transparent denials to the contrary, his own readers wanted to be kept informed about what was going on in Vienna.

But let us now return to the *Broschürenflut*. Without making the hopeless attempt to produce a systematic analysis of the literally thousands of pamphlets that appeared in Vienna over the span of a decade, copies of most of which are anyway no longer to be found, I shall try to make some generally valid remarks about their content and to support these with some relevant examples. To do more would be, by far, to exceed the historian's responsibility to remain true to his material.[33]

The first category to which these pamphlets should be assigned, vastly preponderant in total numbers, is that of works dealing with various aspects of the religious life. Here we may as well begin with Eybel's *Was ist der Papst?* This was, in the main, a restatement of his previously developed Febronian thesis about the equality of bishops, which he then further expanded in *Was ist ein Bischof?* He went beyond this in *Was ist ein Pfarrer?*, maintaining that in all important considerations the priest was the equal of the bishop, and also demanding that a start be made in granting toleration to other faiths.[34] Sonnenfels himself entered the lists at this point with an attack on Eybel, on the occasion of the visit of Pope Pius VI to Vienna. There was no need, he maintained, for such imprudent and ideological sorties. He himself had seen to it that the enlightenment was so well established in Austria that there could be no further question about

32. *Allgemeine Deutsche Bibliothek*, LI/2 (1782), 561–562.

33. When I have not been able to consult the actual pamphlets, I base my remarks on the extensive summaries which appeared in the *A.D.B.* By the end of 1782 over a thousand pamphlets had been published. See F. Gräffer, *Josephinische Curiosa* (5 vols., Vienna, 1848–50), V, 60.

34. *A.D.B.*, II/2, 562–570.

its eventual triumph. In addition, the Pope would be so astounded by what he observed in Vienna that he would, without further delay, reform his own establishment on the Austrian model.[35] It was not one of the great man's immortal conceits.

Now we come once more to Eybel, whose *Sieben Kapitel vom Klosterleben* inveighs not only against the abuses of monasticism but against the monastic life itself: man is a social being, and it is going against nature to force him to live a solitary life. Moreover, in the early church, monks, whatever good or bad they may have done, at least had not been priests. The combination of the two functions had done positive damage to the church.[36]

An anonymous pamphlet appearing in 1782 strongly supported the intention of Joseph to dissolve a considerable proportion of the monasteries.[37] Another attacked Cardinal Migazzi, telling him that he would do far better to reform the morals of his clergy than to complain about the work of the reformers.[38] Once more Eybel, in *Was ist von Ehedispensen zu halten?*, attacked the system of granting such dispensations as socially discriminatory—the poor simply could not afford to pay for them.[39] And Eybel's *Was enthalten die Urkunden des christlichen Alterthums von der Ohrenbeichte?* finally earned its author the notoriety of having his works pronounced heretical by the papacy. The argument which this little work developed, to the effect that only God can see into the heart of the sinner and forgive him, was, of course, a standard Protestant one.[40]

Closely related to the above were the pamphlets that were concerned specifically with toleration. There was, for instance, an impassioned but historically confused appeal by Heinrich

35. J. v. Sonnenfels, *Ueber die Ankunft Pius VI. in Wien* (Vienna, 1782).

36. *A.D.B.*, LV/1, 267. Nicolai cannot resist adding smugly that these were discoveries that had been made in the Protestant world long ago.

37. *Gedanken über einige dem Publikum sehr nützliche Verbesserungen in Wien* (Vienna, 1782).

38. *A.D.B.*, LVII/2, 557.

39. *Ibid.*, p. 565.

40. *Ibid.*, LXI/2, 526.

Joseph Watteroth,[41] and the published text of a circular letter from Bishop von Hug of Koniggrätz to his clergy, forbidding them to preach sermons in opposition to the principle of toleration.[42] The topic ceased to be actual with the promulgation of Joseph's toleration edicts, in October, 1781, for Protestants and members of the Greek Orthodox confession, and in a more limited sense for the Jews in January, 1782.[43]

A smaller but important category of pamphlets dealt with the even more sensitive subject of the powers of the crown. One such anonymous brochure maintained that the monarch had the right to prevent, by force if necessary, the publication of papal bulls in his territories, as these might lead to grave disorders.[44] Another, longer, document in the form of a *roman à clef* praised Joseph and all his works.[45] A third gave him gratuitous advice on how better to enforce his reform program, given the not inconsiderable opposition of his ungrateful subjects.[46] Yet another was a sharply drawn critique by Baron Friedrich von der Trenck of the new legislation affecting the peasantry. This argued that it would do no good to abolish serfdom: while this would contribute to the impoverishment of the nobility, it would in no way reduce its arrogance, and the peasants would anyway not be inclined to work any harder.[47]

All this was possible because Joseph, who did not in the least

---

41. H. J. Watteroth, *Für die Toleranz überhaupt und Bürgerrecht der Protestanten in katholischen Staaten* (Vienna, 1781).

42. *A.D.B.*, LI/2, 598.

43. On the toleration patents see G. Frank, *Das Toleranz-Patent Kaiser Josephs II.* (Vienna, 1882); my "Joseph II and the Jews: The Making of the Toleration Patent of 1782," *Austrian History Yearbook*, IV/V (1970); and C. H. O'Brien, *Ideas of Religious Toleration at the time of Joseph II: A Study of the Enlightenment among Catholics in Austria, Transactions of the American Philosophical Society*, N.S., LIX/7 (1969).

44. *Ueber das Recht des Landesfürsten in Betreff der dogmatischen Bullen* (Vienna, 1781).

45. *Die Gimpelinsel, oder der Stiefbruder des Linnäus* (Vienna, 1782).

46. *Vorschlag eines patriotischen Oesterreichers für Joseph II.* (Vienna, 1782).

47. F. v. der Trenck, *Meine Gedanken über die unsichtbare Leibeigenschaft des Königreichs Böhmen* (Vienna, 1782).

like outsiders to concern themselves with the business of government, had nevertheless decided as early as 1781 that attacks upon him and his administration were to be permitted. This decision had been made initially with reference to a pamphlet by one Steinberg, entitled *Briefe aus Berlin*, which combined a bitter attack on the person of the Emperor for retaining any censorship at all with a complaint about the administration of one of his favorite public projects, the Vienna poorhouse: not only were the inmates put on a near-starvation diet, as the sum of eight kreutzer a day per head allotted for their sustenance was grossly insufficient, but the directors even expected to get some work out of these poor wretches. When the Censorship Commission proposed to ban the offending pamphlet, Joseph replied that the administrators of the *Armeninstitut* would have to consider themselves repaid for the insults they had been subjected to by having had their names paired with his, and that anyway it was well known that only good and important things were attacked in the press.[48] As a result, at most three or four books were banned by the censorship from the beginning of his reign until the end of 1783.[49] It was, however, possible to go too far. A pamphlet addressing itself to agricultural conditions in Upper Austria complained that the peasants were subject to continual exploitation not only by the naturally rapacious landlords, but by officials of the crown as well. When they objected, it was as difficult for them to get justice in the newly reformed courts as it had been in the old manorial ones. The censorship would not permit this pamphlet to be printed in Austria, and it finally appeared outside the borders of the monarchy.[50] In general,

48. Sashegyi, *Zensur und Geistesfreiheit*, pp. 108–109; Mitrofanov, *Joseph II*, 789.

49. Sashegyi, *Zensur und Geistesfreiheit*, p. 116. In 1782 Hume's *Dialogue Concerning Natural Religion*, which had long been banned, was admitted to circulation on the strength of the argument that it was so boring that no one aside from a professional academician could ever get through it.

50. *A.D.B.*, LVII/2 607: *Behandlung oberensischer Unterthanen zur Beherzigung für meine Freunde, und wollte Gott auch für Joseph II.*

Joseph was more sensitive to attacks on his system than to those directed against himself. This would seem to be borne out by his insistence that a brochure entitled *The Forty-two-Year-Old Ape*, which appeared in the year in which he reached that age, be passed in spite of the fact that, aside from depicting him as a semi-literate who spouted political maxims that he didn't understand, it denigrated Austria as a citadel of hedonism—a *Fressland* too deeply concerned with satisfying its vulgar material needs to harbor true art and literature.[51] Joseph is said to have observed at the time that he would let anyone write what he pleased, so long as in turn he was permitted to do as he pleased.

The rest of the *Broschürenflut* can be classed, along with the already mentioned chambermaid literature, as trivia. One example must suffice: a work defending the tailors of Vienna against overcharging and shoddy workmanship. The real culprits were the fine gentlemen of the town who thought nothing of ordering several expensive suits of clothes without ever intending to pay for them.[52] This may have been social criticism, but hardly of a very high order.

A curious offshoot of the rage to publish was a journal, founded in 1871, with the promising title of *Wöchentliche Wahrheiten für und über die Prediger in Wien*. The idea was genial: reporters were sent into the principal churches of Vienna on Sundays, and abstracts of the sermons preached were published, along with critiques; eventually a system of assigning grades to sermons was devised, based on how closely they conformed to the spirit of the Josephinian reforms. The Archbishop protested against this at length and repeatedly, but to no effect.[53]

As the flood of publications would not stop, because the pub-

---

51. *Der 42. jährige Affe. Ein ganz vermaleidetes Märchen* (Berlin [Prague], 1784).

52. *Gute Nacht, oder Vertheidigung der äusserst verletzten Ehre der bürgerlichen Schneider in Wien* (Vienna, 1781).

53. K. Strasser, "Die 'Predigerkritiken': Ein Beitrag zur Geschichte des Josephinismus," *Jahrbuch des Vereines für Geschichte der Stadt Wien*, XI (1954), 104–110.

lic, although continuing to be unpredictable in its tastes, kept on buying most of what appeared for sale in the stalls, Joseph decided that some sort of brake would have to be put on. In May, 1784, a new regulation was introduced, decreeing that henceforth anyone wishing to publish a work of less than 150 pages would have to deposit the sum of six ducats with the censors. Should the pamphlet be turned down, the money would be forfeit.[54] This might have achieved its desired effect and stemmed the flood to some extent, not so much because the danger of losing the deposit was great, the censorship still being relatively lax, but rather because most pamphleteers did not dispose over six ducats in liquid assets. At the last minute, however, Joseph changed his mind and restricted himself to giving instructions to the censors to administer the existing regulations more vigorously.

The *Broschürenflut* was characterized by a remarkable preponderance of chaff over wheat. The rush into print was too precipitate, the need to catch the latest wind of fashion too pressing, for real substance to emerge. Problems, some real, some frivolous, were touched on ever so lightly before other topics demanded the attention of the starveling authors who wrote the great bulk of the pamphlets. Only one subject was thoroughly aired: anti-clericalism, which could always be depended on to sell, and which, to a degree, corresponded with government policy and was thus perfectly safe. Even there, no great advances were made. The state of the art as it had developed in this period is summed up in Eybel's major and final statement, the *Briefe aus Rom über die Aufklärung in Österreich*.[55] This is an extremely broad satire, purporting to be the outraged protest of

54. The text of the decree is in Kink, *Kaiserlichen Universität*, I/2, 286. In the preamble this step is justified on the following ground: "Da . . . der Beweis klar vorhanden lieget, dass unendlich viel Broschüren geschmieret werden, und schier keine einzige noch an das Tageslicht gekommen ist, die der hiesigen Gelehrsamkeit Ehre gemacht oder dem Publico einige Belehrung verschaffet hätte. . . ." See also Brunner, *Mysterien der Aufklärung*, p. 103.

55. J. V. Eybel (Zakkaria), *Briefe aus Rom über die Aufklärung in Oesterreich* (Frankfurt a. M. and Leipzig, 1785).

an obscurantist priest about the recently introduced church reforms. Just when it had appeared that at long last blind faith was about to triumph over all its enemies, Joseph had been seized with the unhappy notion of introducing light into regions where hitherto darkness had reigned supreme. The result was that at present priests were no more believed by their flocks than were the rabbis when they told the Jews about the imminent coming of the Messiah. The innumerable dogmas so painstakingly invented and fraudulently introduced at great expense by the church no longer found credibility among the mass of believers. The truth could appear in print, at a price every man was able to afford. Sums of money so lovingly hoarded by generations of monks were used for such scandalously nonreligious purposes as the feeding of the poor. The Jesuits, once the ornament of the church, had been reduced to poisoning the last pope (Clement XIV) in order to gain revenge for the dissolution of their Society. And much more in the same vein.[56] On balance, one is inclined to prefer the polemics of the Protestant Reformation, which at least had a certain freshness about them.

The chief importance of the *Broschürenflut* was that it both provided an opportunity for young writers to learn the rudiments of their trade and helped to create a taste for more serious, more studied, more formal literature.

56. *Ibid.*, pp. 2, 4, 6–7, 18, 25, 88, 108.

4
Masons and Bards

IN 1781 an imperial edict decreed that thereafter no societies within Austria would be permitted to function if they
continued to recognize a foreign head. The law was aimed at
monastic orders and ecclesiastical societies, but it was worded
so that secular organizations were affected by it as well. The result was that the Austrian Masonic lodges, which up until that
time had been subject to the authority of the Grand Lodge of
Berlin, suddenly were left to their own devices.[1] In the ensuing
scramble there was a perhaps inevitable loss of discipline and
cohesion, factionalism caused new lodges to split away from established ones, and for a time it appeared that the Masons would
lose, if not the majority of their members, surely their effective
leaders to the newly created Order of the Illuminati. Founded
by the ex-Jesuit Adam Weishaupt in Bavaria in 1776, this society was organized along lines which were the result of the
founder's experience in the Society of Jesus. It had for its modest
goal the eventual rationalization of all human activity. This
undeniably laudable purpose was to be accomplished by gathering together influential men of good will wherever they could
be found. As the number of such persons was necessarily limited,
this necessitated drawing upon the Masons. From the time of
their foundation, the Illuminati were reputed to support arcane
and dangerous doctrines, possibly even republicanism. All other

1. Lennhoff, *Die Freimaurer*, p. 181.

things being equal, they would undoubtedly have been suppressed by the Austrian police, even under Joseph II, except that Joseph entertained vague hopes, both before and after the War of the Bavarian Succession (1778–79), that the order would support him in his attempts to add Bavaria to his dominions. In consequence, the Illuminati were allowed to organize and function in Austria, and for a time attracted such Masonic luminaries as Sonnenfels into their ranks.[2]

The Illuminati, however, proved to be even more vulnerable than the Masons to factionalism and petty disputes, and long before they were suppressed in 1784 most of their membership had been reabsorbed by the Masonic lodges. I have already argued that Masonry was a coat of many colors. But insofar as any one lodge can be identified with the subject of this study, the literary enlightenment and its political content, this was *Zur wahren Eintracht*, founded in 1781 by fifteen dissidents who had left the older *Zur gekrönten Hoffnung*. The original founders were not men of remarkable abilities or connections, but they were joined in the following year by Ignatz von Born, who in short order succeeded in transforming the lodge into the equivalent of a fashionable club for supporters of the enlightenment.[3]

Born in 1742 into a family of Transylvanian gentry, Ignatz von Born was intended for the Society of Jesus. He left the Jesuits after a year and a half and began to study law at Prague. This did not suit him either, and he changed careers once more, embarking upon a course of study in natural philosophy, particularly mineralogy and geology. In 1770 he was employed to conduct a mineralogical survey of a part of Hungary, including Transylvania. His published reports of his findings, although

2. L. Engel, *Geschichte des Illuminaten-Ordens* (Berlin, 1906), pp. 193–196; E. F. S. Hanfstaengl, *Amerika und Europa von Marlborough bis Mirabeau* (Munich, 1930), pp. 135–160. See also my *Joseph II and Bavaria* (The Hague, 1965); and Abafi, *Freimaurerei*, VI, 130–132.

3. Abafi, *Freimaurerei*, IV, 278–280. For Born see Zellwerker, *Ignaz von Born, passim*; and Wurzbach, *Biographisches Lexicon*, II, 71.

they necessarily concern themselves with what was to be found beneath the soil, show that he was by no means blind or indifferent to what he observed on the surface. For instance, he comments with evident approval on his host of an evening, a lieutenant colonel commanding an Illyrian regiment on the frontier. This officer had made efforts to introduce more genteel standards of behavior among his subordinates, made every attempt to humanize the lives of the private soldiers under his command, and had even seen to it that schools for their children were established. Born describes with distaste the hordes of convicts, chained together and racked by swamp fever, who can every day be seen marching along the roads. He comments on the ignorance, the perpetually besotted state, but also the real misery of the peasants.[4] He gives numerous indications that he is possessed of a highly developed social conscience.

In 1771 Born wrote a satirical piece, *Die Staatsperücke,* lampooning the mindless insistence on empty formalism prevalent among government officials. Later he was to contribute to the flood of pamphlets with an effort entitled *Specimen monachologiae methodo Linnaeana,* which painstakingly classified the various orders of monks on the evolutionary scale, in the hitherto unfilled space between the higher apes and man.[5]

Born had been brought to Vienna to classify and preside over the imperial mineral collection. After 1782 his real passion, however, was without doubt his lodge. Having been elected president of *Zur wahren Eintracht,* he devoted his efforts to spreading enlightenment wherever possible, to the difficult task of trying to achieve harmony among the forever quarreling members of the intelligentsia, and to putting to use funds supplied by the wealthier members of the lodge in the good work of supporting the poorer among the literati.[6] Nor did he confine his patronage

4. I. v. Born, *Travels through the Bannat of Temesvar, Transylvania and Hungary in the Year 1770,* trans. R. E. Raspe (London, 1777), pp. 10–17.
5. R. Keil, *Wiener Freunde, 1784–1808* (Vienna, 1883), p. 8.
6. D. Silagi, *Jakobiner in der Habsburger-Monarchie* (Vienna and Munich, 1962), p. 42.

exclusively to writers. Austrian musicians, although more likely to be able to support themselves by their professional work than writers, were nevertheless frequently in need of assistance, and Born did what he could for them. For instance, he introduced Joseph Haydn into his lodge as a full-fledged member, and was helpful to him in other ways. However, the story which one frequently encounters, to the effect that the members of the lodge, having for years subsidized Mozart and having at last seen themselves repaid with the appearance of *The Magic Flute*, proceeded to poison him because he intended to desert the Masons for the Rosicrucians and to denounce his opera as a work of Masonic propaganda wrung from him against his will, is utter fantasy, totally inconsistent with what is known of the characters of the men involved.[7]

For the most part, however, Born supported writers, some of whom became members of the lodge while others were merely assisted when their work seemed to be in the general interest of the Masons. Never closer than the periphery of this circle, never a Mason, yet entertaining close relations with many members of Born's lodge, was Michael Denis, regarded by the majority of his contemporaries as the leading poet of the age. Born in Upper Austria in 1729, educated by the Jesuits, he had become a member of the Society in 1756. Eventually he became a teacher of literature in the Theresianum in Vienna. His main interest was English literature, which led him in 1768 to produce a translation of the *Songs of Ossian*. This collection of ancient Celtic lays had, in actuality, been written by the eccentric Scot James MacPherson, who chose to pass them off as the work of Ossian, son of Fingal, saying he had discovered them in a remote archive, and thus perpetrated one of the most successful literary forgeries of all time. The murky, secretive, precultural tone of the poems, evocative of a dim but appealing Germanic past, acted powerfully

---

7. A. Bartels, *Freimaurerei und deutsche Literatur* (Munich, 1929), pp. 59–62. This book is essentially a National Socialist attack on the Masons, but the story in question has a wide circulation.

on many German intellectuals, whose descendants would, a generation later, lose themselves in a cult of similar romantic flummery. Denis produced a great deal of bardic poetry of his own, none of it on the level of *Ossian*. He never deserted the Jesuits in spirit, as so many of his contemporaries were to do. As late as 1790 he published a poem lamenting the lost fellowship of the Society—never would men be tied to one another with such bonds of love again.

Yet Denis adapted to the changes that he was forced to live through. At the Theresianum he taught a seminar in literary history which soon became known for its free-wheeling methods and its willingness to tackle any subject. When the Theresianum was closed down in 1783, he was taken on as a court librarian, a desirable sinecure, through the influence of Kaunitz, ordinarily no lover of Jesuits. While remaining, insofar as he dared, true to his past, Denis embraced a position which came to be characteristic for the Austria of his day: reform Catholicism, a clerical version of reform conservatism. He did not himself press for changes, but refrained from objecting to those that came, and even approved of those which he did not regard as fatal to the interests of the church. He was a transitional figure.[8]

A very similar type was Karl Joseph Michaeler, who after the dissolution of the Jesuits became professor of universal history at the University of Innsbruck. There he translated Schlötzer's *World History* into Latin for use in the Austrian universities. In his lectures he made every effort to steer a middle course between clerical reaction and Josephinian liberalism. After Joseph had reduced the University of Innsbruck to a secondary school and Michaeler once again found himself without a job, he gave in to the spirit of the times. He became a Mason, on the strength

8. For Denis see Fischer-Colbrie, *Michael Denis*, pp. 19–23; Mühlher, "Literatur der Aufklärung," p. 294; Nadler, *Literaturgeschichte*, pp. 184–189; Nagl, Zeidler, and Castle, *Literaturgeschichte*, II, 43–46, 76–78; Wurzbach, *Biographisches Lexicon*, III, 39; P. v. Hofmann-Wellenhof, *Michael Denis* (Innsbruck, 1881), *passim*; and J. J. Daly, "The Poet of a Lost Camelot," *Thought*, XIII (1938), 412.

of the connections thus obtained got a job in the library of the
University of Vienna, and thereupon wrote a pamphlet defending the validity of secretly contracted marriages of priests, as
these would anyway soon be legalized by the abolition of sacerdotal celibacy.[9]

If Denis refused to break completely with his past, the same
cannot be said of Alois Blumauer. Born in Steyer, Upper Austria,
in 1755, educated in a Jesuit school, he entered the Society as a
novice, only to be thrown out on the street a year later at the
time of the dissolution. For some years his existence seems to
have been extremely precarious. There is reason to believe that
he made ends meet by serving as a police spy.[10] He may have
briefly held posts as tutor and private secretary. He first emerged
from the obscurity of the Viennese demimonde in 1780, when
he found regular employment as a supernumerary cataloger in
the court library, then being reorganized by Gottfried van Swieten. Shortly thereafter he submitted a play as an entry in a competition organized by the Burgtheater. Although nothing more
than an exiguous imitation of Goethe's *Goetz von Berlichingen*,
it was nevertheless given a prize and put into production. Blumauer's career as a literary figure was now launched.[11] His poetry
and his political opinions were now no longer merely the effusions of yet another inhabitant of Grub Street, but would find a
ready outlet. His first efforts after his triumph were, not too
surprisingly, a number of attacks on his fellow authors.

First in a satirical poem, then in an essay, Blumauer held
the literary lions of the *Broschürenflut* up to merciless ridicule.
No subject had proved too trivial for them to take up; they wrote
only in order to make money; their pitiful products were written
in a day, read the next, forgotten the third. They created the most
unfortunate impression abroad; the entirely laudable lifting of

9. Wolfsgruber, *C. A. K. Migazzi*, p. 832.
10. Wurzbach, *Biographisches Lexicon*, I, 436; G. Gugitz, "Alois Blumauer,"
J.G.G., XVIII (1908), 35.
11. Gugitz, "Alois Blumauer," pp. 37–38.

the censorship had produced the meagerest of results.[12] It was not a bad day's work. At one and the same time Blumauer deprecated his competitors, called attention to his own superior critical acumen for the benefit of north German reviewers, and registered his enthusiastic approval of Joseph's reforms. Having thus given ample proof of his liberal credentials, the ex-Jesuit novice did not fail to be rewarded. At the end of 1781 he was appointed co-editor of the *Wiener Musenalmanach*, a literary journal that had enjoyed a modest success since its inception four years before. Shortly thereafter he became editor-in-chief of the *Wiener Realzeitung*, which had been started some ten years before as a business paper, but had evolved into yet another literary journal. Blumauer used its pages for a vigorous campaign in support of Joseph's toleration policies and as a vehicle for attacks against not only the clerical obscurantists but also the Jansenists, whose partial reform program he regarded as wholly inadequate.[13]

In 1782 Blumauer was appointed to the Educational Commission, which had just been put in charge of administering the censorship. He was thus obviously in an excellent position to further and protect his own work, an opportunity of which he made frequent and regular use. His next venture into journalism came in 1784, when, at the urging of Sonnenfels and Born, he was appointed editor of the newly founded *Journal für Freymaurer*. As envisaged by its founders, the purpose of this publication was to be the education of the general public about the real purposes of Masonry. The quarrels of Masons, Illuminati, and Rosicrucians, accompanied as they were by completely unrestrained recriminations, had resulted in a suspicion of the motives of all secret societies, and it was judged advisable to make an attempt to dispel whatever unfortunate impressions had been

12. A. Blumauer, *Sämtliche Werke* (9 vols., Munich, 1827), VIII, 59–93. See also Gugitz, "Alois Blummauer," pp. 43–44; and K. Bulling, *Johann Baptist von Alxinger* (Leipzig, 1914), p. 11.

13. Lennhoff, *Die Freimaurer*, p. 184; Gugitz, "Alois Blumauer," pp. 46–47; O'Brien, *Religious Toleration*, pp. 60–61; O. Rommel, "Der Wiener Musenalmanach," *Euphorion*, Ergänzungsheft VI (1906), 9–10.

formed. Blumauer, however, filled the pages of the journal with strident arguments on behalf of the Masons, expositions of the views held by his lodge in contrast to those of others, and so in all probability frustrated the purpose for which it had been intended.[14]

In the meantime he had achieved fame far beyond the reach of mere journalism with the appearance of his major poem, *A Travesty of the Aeneid*, in 1782. Virgil's rather pompous masterpiece is easy to satirize, and there had been no lack of attempts over the centuries. Blumauer's is chiefly notable for the virulence of its anti-clericalism. He directs his not always well-aimed shafts at monks, Jesuits, the Inquisition, the cult of relics, unlikely legends about saints, the political ambitions of the church, pilgrimages, and the like. He went much further than anyone in Austria, including Eybel, had dared to go before, and his success was instantaneous. A first edition of 12,000 copies was bought up almost at once, and for the next ten years Blumauer was under pressure from his publisher to produce endless sequels, which, as he lost interest in the subject, he did with growing reluctance.[15] The poem is frequently called the most important document of the Austrian enlightenment. To the extent that it translated the anti-clericalism of a small intellectual elite to the popular level, this may be so. But if enlightenment is more than the promotion of a secular spirit by scurrilous attacks on the church, one may have one's doubts.

Blumauer's anti-clericalism was not even packed away with his winter clothes when he went on holiday. In a poem written while summering in the lovely mountain valley of Gastein, he describes the primitive life of the peasants, their disregard for the elementary rules of sanitation, their dirty appearance and rough demeanor: they were little better than animals. At fault, of course, was the Catholic government of Salzburg, under whose

14. Kuess and Scheichelbauer, *200 Jahre Freimaurerei*, p. 50; Zenker, *Wiener Journalistik*, p. 75.
15. Gugitz, "Alois Blumauer," pp. 49–55.

disreputable and obscurantist rule no other conditions were to be expected.[16]

This does not mean that, at least on occasion, Blumauer was not capable of producing work of a higher order. In the poem *Der reiche Mann*, he complains about the irresponsibility of the rich and about the social system that allows them not only to be ignorant, rude, lazy, immoral, and dishonest, but in addition to have themselves praised for their faults by whatever starveling poets they have succeeded in suborning:

> Wer immer hier auf dieser Welt
> Zu faul zur Arbeit ist
> Und thun nur will, was ihm gefällt,
> Und Andere verdriesst;
> Der werde reich; ein reicher Mann
> Darf alles was er will und kann!
> Denn nur der Reiche kann allein
> Mit guter Art ein Dumkopf seyn.
>
> etc.[17]

In a panegyric about Joseph, Blumauer praised him for being able to discern the good human being in even a Protestant or a Jew; for breaking the chains of the peasant, whose labors would hereafter be on behalf of himself and of his progeny rather than expended on others; for having liberated intelligence, which henceforth would be limited only by the dictates of truth; for having at last achieved a workable separation of church and state; for having put the mighty of both in their places; for having

16. A. Blumauer, *Epistel an meinen Freund Pezzl von Gastein im Salzburgischen.* See also L. Schmidt, "Blumauer und das Volkslied," *Germanisch-romanische Monatsschrift,* XXVIII (1940), 92–93. In fact, at the time of Blumauer's visit, Archbishop Hieronymus Colloredo, a disciple of the enlightenment whose interest in this remote corner of his jurisdiction was enhanced by the fact that he too spent his summers there, was trying desperately to suppress superstition and introduce reforms into the valley, only to be met with the most obstinate refusal on the part of the inhabitants to cooperate. See H. v. Zimburg, *Die Geschichte Gasteins und des Gasteiner Tales* (Vienna, 1948), pp. 205–206; and J. Wodka, *Kirche in Österreich* (Vienna, 1959), p. 300.

17. Blumauer, *Sämtliche Werke,* I, 94–96.

made an end of the monasteries which robbed the country of
badly needed labor; and for not spilling his subjects' blood in
needless wars.[18] Even if not, strictly speaking, accurate, this was
at least a broadly comprehensive appreciation of the Emperor's
work.

Wildly inaccurate, but providing an insight into what was
Blumauer's fundamental commitment, was an ode to Joseph in
his capacity as protector of the Masons:

> Joseph, der so eben von den Horden
> Träger Mönche seinen Staat befreit,
> Schätzt und schützt dafür nur einen Orden,
> Der sich ganz dem Wohl der Menschheit weiht.[19]

Blumauer the aimless drifter had found the home of which the
Jesuits' dissolution had deprived him. Hereafter his importance
lay principally in his role as a propagandist for Masonry. As a
popularizer of the enlightenment, only his *Aeneid* set him apart
from a small crowd of like-minded men, some of whose abilities
by far outstripped his own. As a representative of a new, bourgeois
literature, his position in the bourgeoisie was somewhat too
tenuous to permit much of a case to be made. And to single him
out for particular distinction in the honorable company of parvenu poets is not justified by his meager talent.

The third member of what is generally regarded as the Josephinian triumvirate of letters, Johann Baptist von Alxinger,
lived at the opposite end of the social scale. Born in Vienna in
1755 in genteel surroundings, educated by the Jesuits, he studied
law at the university under Martini and took a doctorate in that
discipline in 1780, but as his not inconsiderable private means
did not put him under the obligation of making a living, he
never entered upon the practice of law. Instead, he was to spend
most of his life in close association with playwrights, poets, and
pamphleteers, and himself became, perhaps because he did not

---

18. *Ibid.*, II, 103–106.
19. *Ibid.*, IV, 11–14.

have to be a bureaucrat as well, the ablest of the Josephinian poets.[20]

After 1780 Alxinger divided his time between engaging in discussion with a group of young poets, later to be called the *Wiener Freunde,* Masonic activities, translating librettos and French dramas for the Viennese stage, and attending the daily afternoon gatherings at the Greiners. His marriage to Maria Anna von Wetzlar, whose father was a converted Jew, was very unhappy, and after some years of private misery and public scandal he packed her off to a nunnery. He began to publish poems fairly regularly in the *Musenalmanach* and the *Realzeitung,* and, in spite of the fact that his major attempts to storm the Viennese stage remained unsuccessful, established a reputation as one of the better craftsmen among the poets of Vienna.[21]

He also raised his voice loudly and often on behalf of religious toleration. Perhaps because of his marriage connection, he took up the cause of the Jews, not the most popular even among the liberals. In the poem *Lied eines alten Juden,* he spoke to the anti-Semites, asking them whether the Jew had not, like them, been created by God to serve as an ornament to his all-seeing wisdom.[22] Whereas it was perfectly safe to defend that which had already been translated into the law of the land, and all Alxinger risked by speaking out in favor of the Jews was social disapproval, he soon demonstrated that he was willing to go further. One consequence of Joseph's edict of toleration of 1781 had been a great rush away from Catholicism. Particularly in Bohemia, where crypto-Protestantism had been endemic since the forcible re-Catholicization following upon the Czech defeat in 1620, people left the church in droves. By no means happy about what

20. Wurzbach, *Biographisches Lexicon,* I, 22; O'Brien, *Religious Toleration,* pp. 67–69; E. Probst, "Johann Baptist von Alxinger," *J.G.G.,* VII (1897), 172–173; Bulling, *J. B. v. Alxinger,* pp. 1–7.
21. Bulling, *J. B. v. Alxinger,* pp. 8–13; Probst, "J. B. v Alxinger," pp. 174–175.
22. H. Spiel, *Fanny von Arnstein oder die Emanzipation* (Frankfurt a. M., 1962), p. 99.

was to him an unexpected turn of events, Joseph finally established a deadline after which no one would be permitted to do so without going through the most complex formalities, but he accepted what had happened as a fait accompli. But having swallowed the camel, he strained at the gnat. A small group of Czech peasants appeared at the registry office of their village and announced that they wished to be registered as deists. What they meant by this is a matter of conjecture. Certainly what they had in mind had nothing to do with the deism of the French philosophes. They may have been crypto-Adamites, as sects in Bohemia tended to subsist underground for centuries after their supposed disappearances. At any rate, on being informed of this, Joseph ordered that the would-be deists be given two dozen strokes with a cane on their behinds and sent home, and the whole procedure was to be repeated daily until they chose to register as members of one of the major religions.[23]

Alxinger now wrote a seething protest, *Die Duldung*, which van Swieten refused to clear for publication. Undismayed, Alxinger published it abroad in the Leipzig journal *Deutsches Museum*. The thrust of his argument is that mere toleration is not enough; the ruler must grant his subjects full freedom of conscience. Whatever religions they choose to practice must be placed on a completely equal footing. In the tradition of natural law, the prince may be granted rights over the lives and the property of his subjects, but not over their consciences. In addition, compelling people to believe against their wills is just not feasible: the best one can hope to achieve is mass hypocrisy.[24] As was to be expected, this piece contributed heavily to the enhancement of Alxinger's reputation among the Protestant intelligentsia of northern Germany. So did his consistent refusal to identify himself with the Jansenist reformers, whose program

23. Bernard, *Joseph II*, p. 104; R. J. Kerner, *Bohemia in the Eighteenth Century* (New York, 1932), p. 42.

24. Probst, "J. B. v. Alxinger," p. 180; O'Brien, *Religious Toleration*, pp. 67–68.

he regarded as too theistically oriented to achieve worthwhile results and whom he denounced as "Jansenistische Sauertöpfe."[25]

In 1784 Alxinger took a trip to Germany, calling first on Wieland, then on Nicolai. He had been sent to settle some matters affecting his lodge, but apparently he bungled his commission. Shortly after his return to Vienna, following a quarrel of some consequence, he resigned and joined *Zur wahren Eintracht*. Apart from this, he had gathered some impressions in the course of his journey. He came home convinced that with respect to enlightenment, in spite of all the advances of the recent past, Austria was still far behind the Protestant north, and, as an outgrowth of his earlier philo-Semitism, that of all of the German *Aufklärer*, by far the wisest and noblest was Moses Mendelssohn. [26] In 1785 he wrote to Nicolai that it could not be denied that the greater part of what passed for enlightened thought had originated in the Protestant countries, and moreover was ideologically directly opposed to Catholic doctrine.[27] But if he was reluctant to come to the defense of Catholicism, he was still an Austrian patriot. When Nicolai answered with the sort of blanket denunciation of Austrian Catholicism as nothing better than obscurantism incarnate which had become the stock-in-trade of north German political journalism, Alxinger objected that in Catholic Austria there could be found greater generosity with respect to the toleration of minority religions than in any other European state, with the possible exception of Russia or Prussia.[28]

But whatever changes in Alxinger's opinions may have been the result of his visit to Germany, an evident result of the trip was a drastic change in his life-style. He returned convinced that his efforts had so far been insufficient, that he had not been

25. Werner, *Aus dem Josephinischem Wien*, p. 14.

26. Probst, "J. B. v. Alxinger," pp. 176–177; Bulling, *J. B. v. Alxinger*, pp. 13–15; G. Wilhelm, "Briefe des Dichters Johann Baptist von Alxinger," *Sitzungsberichte der philosophisch-historischen Classe der kaiserlichen Akademie der Wissenschaften, Wien*, CXL (1899), p. 12.

27. Alxinger to Nicolai, April, 1785, Wilhelm, "Alxinger Briefe," p. 15.

28. Alxinger to Nicolai, July 29, 1785, *ibid.*, p. 19.

faithful to his muse, that what he owed to himself at this stage of his career was to produce some major works of poetry. This intention was translated into reality in 1786, when, having made the acquaintance of the Leipzig publishing giant G. J. Göschen, and having impressed the great man with his abilities, he received the assurance that a poetic work of whatever length or type which he would care to submit would be published by that prestigious house.[29] This is not without importance, because it is doubtful whether Trattner, who did not exactly go in for prestige publications, would have taken a risk in bringing out what Alxinger was now proposing to write. Whether any of the smaller Viennese printers would have disposed over the means to do so is highly questionable. What Alxinger had in mind was nothing less than a knightly epic. How the reading public would respond to this was highly problematical.

In 1786 *Doolin von Mainz* appeared. The poem recounts the adventures of yet another of Charlemagne's supposititious paladins. After wading through its seemingly endless succession of formal, awkward stanzas, contemporary reviewers were agreed that the key question was whether the poem was longer than it was boring, or whether the reverse was true. What was universally overlooked was that, well hidden in all but impenetrable thickets of aristocratic flimflam, there were potent political arguments to be found. No longer is the enlightened despot appealed to as the never-failing panacea for all of mankind's ills. Quite to the contrary, the cure can be worse than the disease:

> . . . und Könige; die letzteren wurden zwar
> Als Arzenei der Menschheit angerathen,
> Doch sind sie ärger oft, als selbst das Uebel war.[30]

In fact, genuine wisdom is very seldom to be found in close proximity to princely thrones.[31] In addition, Alxinger touches upon a theme to which he would return with greater emphasis later:

29. Bulling, *J. B. v. Alxinger*, pp. 36–57.
30. J. B. v. Alxinger, *Doolin von Mainz* (Leipzig, 1786), VI/p. 63.
31. *Ibid.*, VI/p. 65.

the course of history is not randomly determined. What happens is the result of immutable laws, operating far below the surface of observable events:

> Streicht überhaupt aus euern Wörterbüchern
> Das Wörtchen Zufall weg; denn alles was geschiet
> Geschiet nach heiligen, ewig sichern
> Gesetzen, wenn man gleich nicht stets das Triebrad sieht.[32]

It was a position compatible both with the traditional eschatology of the past and with the historicism of the future, as well as with the purely mechanistic determinism of some of the philosophes. For this reason it is easy to make far too much of it. But if looked at from a political point of view, it does seem to do away with the proposition that the intervention from above, the will of the prince, is decisive.

Theme and subject matter of *Doolin* were characteristic of a transformation within Alxinger. He was increasingly identifying with his aristocratic heritage. He began to attack Blumauer, not only for his slovenly work and for the general shabbiness of his behavior, but because, as he now saw it, these were the regrettable but inevitable consequences of his having grown up and for a long time lived at the bottom of the social ladder.[33] He had some second thoughts about his previous identification of the enlightenment with a Protestant environment, writing to Nicolai that the campaign of vilification carried on against Austria in the journals of Prussia was nothing less than bigotry and religious hatred elevated to the level of national policy.[34] He even re-examined his commitment to Free Masonry. Whereas in 1784 he had written a number of effusive poems full of uncritical praise for the high ideals and probity of the Masons, in 1788 he warned against accepting Masonic charlatanism, which made up a by no means insignificant proportion of the activities which

32. *Ibid.*, VI/p. 68.
33. Wilhelm, "Alxinger Briefe," p. 31; Bulling, *J. B. v. Alxinger*, p. 61.
34. Alxinger to Nicolai, December 8, 1787, Wilhelm, "Alxinger Briefe," p. 36.

the order engaged in, as an earnest of genuine enlightenment.[35] Doolin is still a Mason, a man of infinite good will and noble heart, who gladly gives of himself in the support of causes that profit his fellow man. But he does so not out of any artificially fostered sense of social obligation, but rather because his nature, the whole of his background, will not allow him to do otherwise. His is an unmistakably aristocratic ideology.[36]

This theme, along with others, is carried further along in Alxinger's next major work, the knightly epic *Bliomberis*.[37] Alxinger worked for some four years on the composition of this poem. In the first instance, it was meant to be a refutation of the critics who had attacked *Doolin* for its stylistic deficiencies, and because the hero of that previous epic had forever been taking part in apparently senseless physical encounters. The new poem was written with the utmost care, verging on pendantry, for the rules of formal philology. Not a single word went into it which Alxinger had not first made sure of as belonging to the vocabulary of literary German rather than to the Viennese dialect. Unfortunately, these scholarly exertions were not matched by an equivalent growth in Alxinger's gift for epic poetry. It was easier to remedy the second fault. Bliomberis was made to undergo not physical but moral tests. Again unfortunately, what this noble resolve produced was a hero whose confused and all but nonsequential actions were scarcely made more intelligible for resulting from insufficiently exposed abstract principle.[38]

Apart from this, *Bliomberis* developed a number of parallel themes. As Alxinger had written to a friend in 1788, the poem was to be a refutation of the iniquitous philosophy of Spinoza and a reaffirmation of the existence of God.[39] As things turned out, either the Talmudic sage proved to be too slippery an an-

35. Rommel, "Musenalmanach," p. 174.
36. R. Bauer, "Les Épopées de Johann Baptist von Alxinger," *Études Germaniques*, VI (1951), 187.
37. J. B. v. Alxinger, *Bliomberis* (Leipzig, 1791).
38. Probst, "J. B. v. Alxinger," pp. 187–190.
39. Alxinger to Borié, March 12, 1788, Wilhelm, "Alxinger Briefe," p. 46.

tagonist for Alxinger's theological abilities, or in the course of writing his poem he became even more incensed with Spinoza's latter-day imitators, because in fact Bliomberis incorporates an unmistakable attack on the skepticism of David Hume, and on Voltaire.

On a journey to Africa to liberate his father, who has come into the possession of the Holy Grail but has unfortunately been captured by savages, Bliomberis stops off in a country of unbelievers. Skepticism is the law of the land. Even the sixteen-year-olds belittle religion with a supercilious smile, while admitting that it may have its uses as a restraint on the mass of the common people. There are no concerns beyond those of hedonism and only physical love is thought important. The praise of one's contemporaries is valued sufficiently to serve as an acceptable replacement for the eternal life which has been sacrificed to unbelief. This is a cold and sterile environment, where pure intellect can produce nothing more edifying than the cult of the material, and the soul cannot thrive.[40] This argument represents a clear break with the Masonic morality to which Alxinger had previously subscribed—a morality at whose core was a blend of eudaemonism and altruism, a morality based on the proposition that one's own advantage and that of others are linked inextricably, and that to work for the one is to achieve the other.[41]

Underlying the whole work is the subsidiary theme of illegitimacy. Bliomberis, who displays the bar sinister on his shield, struggles throughout the poem to overcome this handicap. It was a subject that Sonnenfels had often touched upon in his lectures. However, Bliomberis' eventual triumph seems to be less the confirmation of the proposition that a man's origins, no matter how unfortunate, should not be held against him, than an argument to the effect that true nobility will be vindicated no matter what the obstacles.

Of more immediate interest is the further development of

---

40. Bulling, *J. B. v. Alxinger*, pp. 101–102; Alxinger, *Bliomberis*, V, 3–6.
41. Bauer, "Les Épopées," p. 190.

Alxinger's by now Montesquieuan political opinions. In a manner reminiscent of the traditions of the mirrors of princes, he defines the rights and obligations of sovereigns. Their subjects must never forget that the person of a ruler is sacred. They are not in the best position to pass judgment on his actions, because his true motives are by no means always apparent to the observer from below. Moreover, no one can please everybody. The monarch is not infallible, much less so as he has from the cradle been exposed to nothing but flattery and self-seeking; if he errs, his subjects must learn to forgive. Even should the prince prove to be a tyrant, his misdeeds should be borne patiently. All rapid change is destructive to society. The worst of rulers in a long reign cannot do so much harm as a rebellion can achieve in the course of a few days.[42] What Alxinger has in mind, however, is no mere rationalization of despotism, enlightened or not. Having reassured whatever interested monarchs might be reading his poem that he is neither a rebel nor a regicide, he goes on to develop his real point: there are limits to a people's patience. A tyrant who spills the blood of his people, who breaks faith with them, has forfeited his right to rule:

> Erbt man ein freies Volk wie eine Heerde Vieh,
> Damit man ungestraft es nach Gefallen schlachte?
> Der Fürst der seiner Nation
> Nicht Treue hält, verwirkt was sie geschworen,
> Sein Recht zu herrschen ist verloren
> Und ledig des Tyrannen Thron.[43]

Both parties to the social contract thus have obligations. But even so, it is not up to the people to divest themselves of even an odious tyrant. They must act through the person of the hero, not quite deus ex machina, but very evidently much more than just another member of a disgruntled mob.[44] Presumably God, in his infinite wisdom, will see to it that a Bliomberis is always

42. Alxinger, *Bliomberis*, VIII/pp. 80–84.
43. *Ibid.*, IX/p. 20.
44. *Ibid.*, IX/p. 62.

available in case of need. Nevertheless, considering that the poem appeared after the death of Joseph II, at a time when not only the censorship laws but also the general mood of the realm had undergone a marked transformation, not in the least because of developments reported from France, it took considerable courage to go through with the publication of these lines.

A further proof of Alxinger's political courage was the part he played in the polemical arguments involving L. A. Hoffmann, a one-time Josephinian publicist who, sensing a change in the wind after the Emperor's death, published a series of scurrilous attacks on his former associates and warned the new Emperor Leopold II that the free-thinkers were fomenting a conspiracy against him. Alxinger published a vigorous refutation of these absurd charges.[45] After Leopold's death in 1792 the political atmosphere very definitely did not favor political commentary and Alxinger confined himself to purely aesthetic pursuits. He died in 1794.

Alxinger's aristocratic polity, with its circumscription of the royal power, was not precisely a retrograde movement toward an irretrievably lost feudal past. But neither was it in any sense a political statement acceptable to a despotism, no matter how enlightened. Had it been couched in less murky and obscure terms, it might well have gotten him into serious difficulties. If anything, it was a prefiguration of the political views of the more responsible among the German romantics.

45. J. B. v. Alxinger, *Anti-Hoffmann* (2 vols., Vienna, 1792); Bulling, *J. B. v. Alxinger*, pp. 137–143; Probst, "J. B. v. Alxinger," pp. 194–197. In 1785 Hoffmann had written a play, *Das Werther-Fieber*, which, apart from condemning the overwrought irrationalism of Goethe's hero, celebrated the merits of a wise prior, very obviously Joseph, who ruled his subjects in strict accordance with the dictates of reason. See Gugitz, *Das Wertherfieber*, pp. x–xi.

5

The Paladins of Josephinism: The Moderates

IN 1783 Baron Tobias Gebler was able to write to Friedrich Nicolai that to his knowledge there had never been so complete and rapid a transformation of the essential opinions of a nation as had lately taken place in Austria. This extended all the way down to the most ordinary class of people, whose advanced opinions put to shame those of many an upper-class intellectual who refused to be separated from a hopelessly outmoded past.[1] Making due allowance for the hyperbole imposed by considerations of national pride, it is still possible to conclude that Gebler was telling at least a partial truth. Some three years after Joseph's accession, not only was the spirit of reform still very much in the air, but there had already been enough reforms introduced, and these of a sufficiently fundamental order, to make it appear likely that the whole of society was about to be transformed. And in spite of Joseph's unequivocally expressed distaste for unsolicited advice and gratuitous felicitations, there was no lack of commentators who now came forward to express their approval of what had already been done and to press upon him their views about what still needed to be accomplished. Following his deepest instincts, Joseph would have much pre-

1. Gebler to Nicolai, November 29, 1783. Werner, *Aus dem Josephinischem Wien*, p. 112.

ferred for them to remain silent. From his point of view, they merely called attention unnecessarily to what were already sufficiently vexatious actions of his. However, since in principle he did not wish to suppress their voices, he had no choice but to suffer their support.

These self-appointed spokesmen for Josephinism may conveniently be divided into two groups: those whose ambition was merely to applaud, who were satisfied to see their aspirations realized within the context of enlightened despotism,[2] and those who would ultimately deem themselves wiser than their master, who would not only proclaim the necessity for this or that specific reform, but would come to entertain politically dangerous and advanced notions about procedural improvements that would facilitate the process.

If any generalization is justified about the men in the first category, it is that they were almost to a man young poet-bureaucrats, and that it was not always clear whether they worked at their office jobs so that they would be enabled to write, or whether they wrote in order to be rewarded with better jobs.

The oldest of these writers was Johann Rautenstrauch. Born in Erlangen in 1746, he came to Vienna in 1770. Having studied law, he obtained a position as court factor, but channeled most of his energies into the composition of plays. His first success came in 1773 with the farce *Jurist und Bauer*. This was followed by numerous other productions in the same genre, and soon Rautenstrauch was under contract to write six plays yearly for the Burgtheater. His livelihood was thus assured.[3] From 1775 to 1781 he also edited the *Wiener Realzeitung*. In the early 1780's he began to publish occasional humorous essays, including the

2. This attitude is summed up in the title of an anonymous pamphlet that appeared in Vienna in 1784: *Vorschlag eines patriotischen Oesterreichers für Joseph II. seine Befehle zuverlässig in Erfüllung zu bringen und sein Volk glücklich zu machen.*

3. Wurzbach, *Biographisches Lexicon*, XXV, 61–65; Nagl, Zeidler, and Castle, *Literaturgeschichte*, II, 289–290.

already noted pamphlet on chambermaids, dealing with the morals of the inhabitants of his adopted city, which, it seems, were not always above reproach. At about this time he became something of a popular hero as the result of an affair that had nothing to do with his literary activities. It happened to come to his attention that a man under sentence of death for murder was in fact innocent, and that evidence to this effect had been turned up. He at once presented this intelligence to the appropriate court and achieved a cancellation of the verdict. However, since in his haste to save the victim of this awful judicial error he had, instead of going through the proper channels, made an *Immediateingabe*, that is, presented the evidence directly, he was sentenced to spend three days in jail for contempt of court.[4]

This contretemps caused Rautenstrauch, fairly late in the day, to begin to write about more serious subjects. In 1785 he produced a fantasy in which, having fallen into a deep sleep, he did not awaken until twenty years later, in the year 1805.[5] Joseph was still on the throne, and his reign of a quarter of a century had produced benefits for the whole nation. In particular Vienna had been transformed to its advantage. The medieval walls had all been torn down; shaded avenues, broad and straight, led through the city; the river Wien, formerly always so prone to flooding, had been contained within steep banks and made navigable. The pitting of wild animals was now prohibited, bingo games were forbidden, lawyers were not allowed to exceed a well-publicized tariff in charging their clients, and government employees were provided with uniforms so that they did not themselves have to bear the expense of appearing at their jobs decently dressed.[6]

In 1786 Rautenstrauch wrote a pamphlet purporting to ex-

4. Zellwerker, *Ignaz von Born*, p. 53.
5. J. Rautenstrauch, *Das neue Wien, eine Fabel* (Vienna, 1785).
6. Rautenstrauch apparently himself earned extra money by writing advertisements for the immensely popular animal pittings. See Nagl, Zeidler, and Castle, *Literaturgeschichte*, II, 291.

amine the reasons for the expulsion of the Jesuits from China.[7] It was in fact a fairly unrestrained attack not merely on the clergy, but on Christianity itself. This was too much for the censors, who forbade its distribution. The affair had a curious sequel. Cardinal Migazzi, wishing to impress upon Joseph that the relaxation of the censorship had opened up a bottomless pit, sought to obtain a copy of the pamphlet. Unable to do so, he at last resorted to stealing the only copy that he found, from the top of the chief censor's desk. He showed this to the Emperor, who was properly incensed with the censorship for allowing such vile attacks to circulate. Migazzi did not bother to enlighten him about the details of his having obtained the pamphlet. When, however, Joseph was apprised of the true circumstances, he let loose a tremendous blast at the Cardinal, who was thus caught in his own snare.

Shortly thereafter Rautenstrauch produced a vicious attack on the bookseller Wucherer, his own publisher. Perhaps they had quarreled; at any rate he denounced him as a presumptuous foreigner who dared to abuse the hospitality offered him in Vienna by publishing and distributing countless attacks on the Emperor and his most laudable reform program.[8] Thereafter Rautenstrauch withdrew from the political arena.

Lorenz Leopold Haschka was born in Vienna in 1749. He attended Jesuit schools, became a member of the Society, and was employed as a teacher in the primary grades in Krems. Upon the dissolution of the Society he came to Vienna to seek his fortune. The right doors would not open for him for some time, but in 1777 he succeeded in gaining an entrée to the house of Baron Greiner, whom he told, incorrectly, that he had never taken his vows as a Jesuit. The Greiner connection soon secured him various remunerative positions, including that of curator in

7. J. Rautenstrauch, *Die Verbannung der Jesuiten aus China* (Constantinople, 1785 [Vienna, 1786]) . See also Abafi, *Freimaurerei*, IV, 61–62.

8. J. Rautenstrauch, *Wie lange noch?* (Vienna, 1786), in Gräffer, *Josephinische Curiosa*, III, 64–86.

the university library and a professorship of aesthetics at the Theresianum.[9] Up to the point of this rather dramatic change in his fortunes, Haschka had attempted to make his way by writing pious poetry that befitted his condition of ex-Jesuit and which, he hoped, would bring him to the favorable attention of Maria Theresa. He had been disappointed in this expectation. Under Greiner's influence he joined the Masons, and what he now began to publish differed materially from his youthful efforts. His poetic denunciations of tyranny now became so unreservedly daring that, in the by no means permissive atmosphere of Maria Theresa's last years, as Haschka continued to go unpunished, there were those who maintained that the only possible explanation was that he was serving as an *agent provocateur* for the police. No evidence to confirm such a hypothesis has, however, come to light.[10]

Haschka's real talent, as was revealed in the following years, was for the composition of occasional pieces, poems two or three pages in length, celebrating great events. His speed, and that of his publishers, was phenomenal. No sooner was a battle fought, or a great man in his grave, than an ode by Haschka immortalizing the event could be bought on every street corner. So he became something of an unofficial poet laureate. Very unofficial, to be sure, because Joseph could not abide him. The imperial displeasure was the consequence of an impertinence that Haschka had permitted himself in 1782. He had published abroad an *Ode to the Emperor*, which, under the pretense of voicing approval of Joseph's religious reforms, was in reality an attack of unmitigated vehemence on the papacy and the person of the Pope. Not satisfied with this, he had then submitted a version of the poem to the

---

9. Wurzbach, *Biographisches Lexicon*, VIII, 20; G. Gugitz, "Lorenz Leopold Haschka," *J.G.G.*, XVII (1907), 38–51; C. Pichler, *Denkwürdigkeiten aus meinem Leben*, ed. E. K. Blümml (2 vols., Munich, 1914), I, 43.

10. Rommel, "Musenalmanach," p. 185. The fact that at least two of his poems resulted in heavy fines for his publisher would seem to speak against such an interpretation of his activities. See Goldfriedrich, *Deutschen Buchhandels*, p. 659.

Austrian censorship, and accompanied it with a fulsome dedication to Joseph. The Emperor was furious and took the unusual step of putting a ban on any and all works, existing and yet to be written, coming from Haschka's pen—a ban which was in effect for over two years.[11] Mozart's sometime librettist, Lorenzo da Ponte, later claimed that it was only because of his intervention that Haschka was not exiled to the distant and unsalubrious Bukowina.

Barred temporarily from adding to his income by writing, Haschka, betraying a certain shallowness in his recently adopted liberal philosophy, borrowed 10,000 florins from his new friend Alxinger in order to invest in what looked like a promising flyer in the slave trade. He was apparently not meant to become the richest poet in the world, because the enterprise he had backed soon failed.[12] When he was once again allowed to publish, Haschka prudently avoided sensitive subjects for some years. But he had always been, if not the first, at least a very early occupant of any bandwagon, and in 1787 he quite correctly detected a trend toward increased political radicalism among some of his literary associates. Encouraged by this, he published a poem attacking, prudently, not Joseph, but the ruler of Hessen, who was notorious for selling his subjects to serve as mercenaries in numerous and obscure wars:

> Pfeiffengequick, Pauken und Trommelgeröll.
> Der Ketten und Pauken Getös
> Und das Brüllen der Gepeitschten
> Ist diesem Landesvater allein Musik.

This was followed by similar and even more outspoken attacks on tyranny and tyrants in the *Journal für Literatur und Völkerkunde*.[13] These would undoubtedly have gotten him into

---

11. Gugitz, "L. L. Haschka," pp. 66, 86; Brunner, *Mysterien der Aufklärung,* pp. 107–109.

12. Gugitz, "L. L. Haschka," p. 56.

13. *Ibid.,* p. 87; H. Voegt, *Die deutsche Jakobinische Literatur und Publizistik* (Berlin, 1955), p. 43.

serious difficulties once more, and, taken by themselves, would have justified his inclusion in the second category of more radical writers, except that they were so clearly an attempt to catch the wind. Even before Joseph's death Haschka had lowered his voice, and afterward he was one of the first to denounce the excesses of the previous reign.

Haschka is best known, however, for one of his occasional pieces. In 1797, with Francis II on the throne, Austria's war against France was not going in the least well. An Austrian army had been forced to capitulate in front of Mantua, and the strains of the Marseillaise were being heard in increasingly uncomfortable proximity to Vienna. Fire could be fought with fire. Joseph Haydn was commissioned to write a hymn to the Emperor and Haschka was the natural choice to write the text. "Gott! erhalte Franz den Kaiser,/ Unsern guten Kaiser Franz" was heard for the first time on February 12, 1797, in the Burgtheater in the Emperor's presence. Haydn's tune was masterful, but Haschka's text, apart from the fact that the meter depended on the Emperor's name (although, as it turned out, with the brief interruption of the period 1835–48, it would have served Austria until 1916), was a colorless blend of adulation and banality, and had later on to be several times revised.[14]

To attack Haschka as a "pious, moralizing ex-Jesuit under Maria Theresia, a free-thinking abbé under Joseph, and a patriotic Tartuffe under Francis"[15] is harsh although not unjust. To denounce him as a mere opportunist who could not wait to howl with the wolves of the counter-revolution when given the chance[16] is to overstate the case. He was evidently not a man of iron resolve. His opinions were all too quickly apt to take on whatever hue would bring him the greatest advantage. But he is not to be confused with men like Hoffmann, who attempted to build new careers in serving as the spokesmen of the Francis-

14. Nagl, Zeidler, and Castle, *Literaturgeschichte*, II, 331–334.
15. Gugitz, "L. L. Haschka," p. 38.
16. Nadler, *Buchhandel*, p. 189.

can reaction. After 1790 his literary friends, far from denouncing him as they had Hoffmann, continued to value his friendship. And throughout his work, diverse as its moods may have been, there is a unifying thread. More than any of his contemporaries, he identifies with Austria, celebrating its unique virtues and, even in a century afflicted with a blindness to externals reminiscent of St. Bernard, its landscape. It thus seems entirely fitting that he should have composed the text of the national hymn.

Entirely atypical was the career of Karl Leonhard Reinhold. Born in Vienna, educated by the Jesuits, he joined the Society in 1772, just in time to be ousted from it in the dissolution. Unable to adjust to the secular world, he joined the Barnabite order in 1774. He blamed himself and his fellow novices for the dissolution, regarding it as God's punishment for their lack of zeal and devotion. As a Barnabite, he proceeded from the study of aesthetics to that of metaphysics, immersing himself so completely in that subject that he brought a spiritual crisis upon himself. He seems to have overcome his doubts sufficiently so that he not only remained in good standing in the order, but in 1780 was entrusted with the responsible position of master of novices. At the same time he was also employed occasionally as a lecturer in philosophy. The lectures he gave were drawn largely from Leibnitz, an ominous sign, which was confirmed shortly afterward when, apparently influenced by the friends of his youth, Alxinger and Blumauer, he joined the Masons. To complete the transformation he also became one of the Illuminati.[17] No more eloquent commentary on the prevailing intellectual atmosphere is required than the fact that membership in these two societies was not regarded as necessarily incompatible with membership in a monastic order.

Shortly thereafter Reinhold, encouraged by his friends and by Denis, began to publish poems attacking religious intolerance

17. Wurzbach, *Biographisches Lexicon*, XXV, 222–230; Keil, *Wiener Freunde*, pp. 2–5; Keil, *Aus klassischer Zeit: Wieland und Reinhold* (2nd ed., Leipzig, 1890), pp. 5–8.

and superstition. His deeper reflections on these subjects led him to the conclusion that both were necessary concomitants of the Catholic religion, and that genuine enlightenment in religion was possible only within the context of Protestantism.[18] This last conclusion may possibly have been abetted by the fact that the young abbé had recently fallen in love with a Viennese beauty. At this point Reinhold discovered that there were, after all, limits to the latitudinarianism with which clerical conduct was viewed in that age. It was definitely not possible to be a monk and a Protestant at the same time. Nor were monks encouraged to marry. Poor Reinhold thus ran afoul of what was unquestionably an anachronism, not to say an affront upon logic: had his monastery been among the hundreds of others dissolved by Joseph, he would have found himself out on the street with the choice of either finding another house to take him in or going his own way in the world, even with the assistance of a grant of money from the government to facilitate his making a new start. As it was, his house was not among those that were dissolved, and, failing dispensations and the permission of his superiors, he could not leave it without subjecting himself to the most severe penalties as a runaway monk.

Thus Reinhold was reduced to making an adventurous flight from Vienna, traveling at night in the disguise of a lady of quality. He reached Leipzig safely and eventually made his way to Weimar, where he was taken in by Wieland. The entire operation had been organized and paid for by the membership of the lodge *Zur wahren Eintracht*. Reinhold made a sufficiently good impression on his host so that Wieland not only agreed to sponsor him among the literati of Germany but also gave him one of his daughters in marriage.[19] Initially, Reinhold thought of himself primarily as a commentator on Austrian affairs, whose disadvantage of being at some distance from the scene of the events he described would be made up for by the greater freedom of

18. Keil, *Wieland und Reinhold*, p. 9.
19. Keil, *Wiener Freunde*, p. 11; Keil, *Weiland und Reinhold*, pp. 8–10.

expression he could allow himself in Weimar. In 1786 he published a series of articles in the *Teutscher Merkur* which, while they commented approvingly on the religious reforms which Joseph had up to that point introduced, pointed out that this work could only come to its proper fruition with the complete triumph of Protestantism over a Catholicism that was manifestly inseparable from obscurantism and repression.[20] These pieces were so badly received in Austria that Reinhold despaired of ever affecting the situation there and turned to other interests. He eventually became one of the leading German philosophers of the second rank, producing sensitive and influential commentaries on the philosophies of both Herder and Kant.[21] Thus a man who would undoubtedly have played a significant role in Austria and who might well have become the foremost commentator on Joseph's reforms was removed from the scene by the mere accident of having belonged to the wrong monastic house.

A much more typical representative of the Josephinian generation of young poets was Franz Xaver Huber. Born in Bohemia sometime after the middle of the century, he arrived in the capital in the late 1770's. Unlike the great majority of his colleagues, he did not succeed in gaining employment with the government, and had to support himself by writing, mainly for the theater. After having had several plays performed in the Josephstadt theater, he produced a novel satirizing the judicial system.[22] His Herr Schlendrian[23] is a judge left over from the old order who, quite out of sympathy with Joseph's new dispensation, so clear that even schoolboys could have interpreted it without being forced to resort to a commentary, decides to uncover the inherent weakness of the new system by rendering absurd decisions. Under

20. "Ehrenrettung der Reformation," *Teutscher Merkur* (1786), #1, pp. 116ff., #2, pp. 42ff.

21. Nadler, *Literaturgeschichte*, pp. 188–189.

22. Wurzbach, *Biographisches Lexicon*, IX, 367–368; Pichler, *Denkwürdigkeiten*, I, 66.

23. F. X. Huber, *Herr Schlendrian, oder der Richter nach den neuen Gesetzen* (2nd ed., Berlin, 1787).

the new laws, a wife was specifically guaranteed her right to her own property as it was defined in the marriage contract. But the husband was also given the right of spending the usufruct of that property so long as the marriage lasted. An irate husband now appeared in Schlendrian's court, complaining that his wife had spent all of her money on hideously expensive ball gowns. Schlendrian decided that even though the form of her investment was unusual, it was up to the husband to display sufficient ingenuity to collect an eminently collectable usufruct therefrom.[24]

The next supplicant was the daughter of a man as well known for his wealth as he was notorious for his parsimony. She had become engaged to be married and her father refused her the dowry which he was by law obliged to provide. Schlendrian ascertains that the father's miserliness is so advanced that he goes about the city in outmoded clothes, patched everywhere, almost rags. His verdict is that no dowry need be provided because another new law holds that in the absence of outer signs of wealth the authorities have no right to suppose its existence.[25]

The following petitioner, also a lady, has no better luck. A recent bride, she complains that her husband has turned out to be impotent and petitions for dissolution of the marriage. Schlendrian reminds her that the law states that there are no grounds for divorce if the impediment to intercourse appears only after the marriage has been concluded. Thus, he rules, it was her responsibility to be better informed beforehand. Moreover, she cannot even be granted legal relief on the ground that she is being deprived of children, as it is an ancient legal principle that an impotent husband is no barrier to the engendering of children.[26] As imbecilic, literal-minded decisions follow one another with relentless regularity, it eventually becomes clear that not only Schlendrian is at fault. The new laws, often hastily drawn up without sufficient regard for the surviving corpus of the old,

24. *Ibid.*, pp. 14–15. The reference is to the General Law Code, par. 89/3.
25. *Ibid.*, pp. 17–20. Cf. par. 55/3.
26. *Ibid.*, pp. 21–34. Cf. par. 46/3.

were often contradictory and unclear.[27] Thus Huber was attacking not only the cantankerous and unreconstructed hangers-on of the old order, but also the precipitate nature of many of the Josephinian reforms.

Johann Friedel was born in Temesvar sometime between 1751 and 1755, the son of a lieutenant serving in a border regiment. Although his father was not a man of means, by dint of considerable sacrifices he managed to send Johann to the Oriental Academy in Vienna, an institution which prepared young men for the consular services. Unfortunately young Friedel was forced to withdraw, whether because of deficient scholarship or conduct is not known. *Faute de mieux*, he entered upon a military career. He served as a cadet for some years, and in 1776 joined an infantry regiment whose colonel was Kornelius von Ayrenhoff, later to achieve fame in the two not habitually related fields of generalship and poetry.

To turn to Ayrenhoff for a moment: although his plays were old-fashioned and didactic in the classical manner, he seems to have harbored opinions which one would not necessarily look for in an eighteenth-century major general. In 1786–87 his duties took him to Görz, where he availed himself of the opportunity to learn more about neighboring Italy. He wrote down his observations in the form of letters addressed to his friend Count Maximilian Lamberg.[28] His impressions of Rome are of particular interest. He traces the (to a German very striking) lack of order, seriousness, and good government that characterizes the eternal city to the circumstance that the popes took over, without subjecting it to anything more than a purely formal process of Christianization, the old Roman policy of *panem et circenses*. The average Roman is additionally tempted to avoid living a solid and productive life by the enormous number of religious

27. *Ibid.*, p. 153. Huber's critique of the regime was apparently developed in his *Der blaue Esel* (Vienna, 1788), a work of which I have been unable to locate a copy.
28. C. v. Ayrenhoff, *Sämmtliche Werke* (4 vols., Vienna and Leipzig, 1789), IV.

holidays, which are nothing less than an opiate depressing human ambition. Worse, hardly a day passes in Rome without at least one murder. The papal government is far too lax in enforcing the law. As Seneca had already pointed out, while a prince who chooses to forgive an attempt on his own life may be setting a splendid example of generosity, he does not have the right to be equally generous with the lives of those he governs. For this reason the work of the otherwise entirely admirable Marchese Beccaria must be called into question. Perhaps the death penalty is a more effective deterrent than is sometimes thought.[29]

The Roman aristocrats come in for a generous measure of criticism. To begin with, many of them are simply too rich. At least a dozen noble families enjoy an income of over 50,000 scudi a year, and this in the midst of general poverty. Such inequity of wealth must be regarded as a great moral evil, far worse than universal poverty. And these aristocrats spend their huge incomes in the most banal way possible, leading lives that would be more suitable to professional hunters or stable-masters, rather than taking the least interest in the arts or in the real world about them. They openly flout the laws of both church and state: although the making of *castrati* is punished by automatic excommunication, there is not a great house in Rome in which these unfortunates do not sing every night, more likely than not in the Pope's presence.[30]

A discussion of Roman education (bad) leads Ayrenhoff into a rather long essay on pedagogy. Rote learning inculcated, inefficiently at that, by monkish teachers succeeds only in burdening the student with the excess baggage of a useless metaphysics and prevents him from developing a capacity for independent thought. Rousseau did not go nearly far enough in his *Émile* in overthrowing the entirely inept and outmoded educational establishment. Ayrenhoff then adds some remarks about philosophy in general, in the course of which he refers to "the masterly

29. *Ibid.*, pp. 38–43.
30. *Ibid.*, pp. 60–72.

Montesquieu" and "the unsurpassed genius Voltaire," in whose hands history for the first time became a meaningful enterprise. He talks about the necessity of supporting a national literature with state money and the duty to teach the national tongue as the first subject in all schools, and closes with a passage full of lavish praise for David Hume.[31] Some of this is good Josephinism, much of it goes rather further.

To return to Friedel: like Sonnenfels, he used the long months of inactivity in which his regiment was in winter quarters to educate himself. Also, he wrote occasional poetry, and an essay about the causes of poverty which unfortunately has not been preserved. In 1778 he obtained his release from the army and for a time worked as a journalist in Troppau in Silesia, just in time to be caught up in the Potato War and arrested by the Prussians as a spy. Upon his release he went to Berlin, but failed miserably in his efforts to storm the literary bastions of that city, being turned away with particular vehemence by Nicolai.[32]

Unrewarding as his stay in Berlin was, it did result in the production of his first serious literary effort, a *Rhapsody to All Friends of Man,* which showed strong traces of the influence of Rousseau. In this piece he attributed the all too familiar shortcomings of human society to the tragic departure from the purity and innocence of the primitive condition, and cast grave doubts on the abilities of the contending schools of metaphysical philosophy to provide effective remedies.[33] Thereafter he turned to the composition of a number of novels, none of which has survived, and only one of which seems to have dealt with social issues, and at that peripherally. This was an *Entwicklungsroman* without any noticeable development, a piece in which the protagonist failed miserably at a seemingly unending series of professions. His misfortunes, apparently, were to be understood as a

31. *Ibid.,* pp. 131–142.

32. Wurzbach, *Biographisches Lexicon,* IV, 357; G. Gugitz, "Johann Friedel," *J.G.G.,* XV (1905), 195–206.

33. Gugitz, "J. F. Friedel," pp. 207–208.

stricture not on him but on society, which was still very much in the tradition of the old baroque *Ständerevue*, a form of social criticism that assumed that all segments of society were hopelessly governed by foolishness, and to which the notion that such a condition was not part of an ordained order and might even be subject to change was quite foreign.[34] Friedel also seems to have tried his luck as an actor, but without much success. In 1781 the death of his father recalled him to Austria, and having settled his affairs, he took up residence in Pressburg. Once established there, he took his revenge for the slights he had suffered in Berlin by publishing a scurrilous account of the literary milieu of that city.[35] In 1783 he joined a troop of actors organized by the celebrated Emanuel Schikaneder, which played frequent engagements at Vienna's Kärntnerthortheater.[36] His appearances in Vienna brought him into contact with the young poets of the capital, and the stimulation of their company led him to resume his career as a writer. As politics was the order of the day, it is hardly astonishing that this was what he chose to write about.

As his maiden effort, Friedel published a collection of letters purportedly written by a young man of fashion in Vienna to his friend in Berlin.[37] The theme of these letters was a fulsome and totally uncritical praise of Joseph, which did not even distinguish between his generalship in the Potato War (undeniably miserable) and his religious policies (at the minimum, vigorous). The only part of the work that can be taken at all seriously is an attack on the censorship in the one area where it was still enormously restrictive, that of morals. Friedel complained that while the ladies of Vienna vied with one another in lowering their *décolletés*, a mere allusion to the female bosom was enough to assure that a work of literature would be banned. The protesta-

---

34. *Ibid.*, pp. 213–214; E. D. Becker, *Der deutsche Roman um 1780* (Stuttgart, 1964), p. 147.

35. J. Friedel, *Briefe über die Galanterien von Berlin* (Gotha, 1782).

36. Gugitz, "J. F. Friedel," p. 221; Nadler, *Literaturgeschichte*, p. 206.

37. J. Friedel, *Briefe aus Wien verschiedenen Inhalts an einen Freund in Berlin* (Pressburg, 1783). Cf. Gugitz, "J. F. Friedel," pp. 224–225.

tions of the clergy that to lower the bars at all would result in an unprecedented wave of crime and public immorality were absurd. Countries with no such prohibitions had no worse crime rates than Austria.[38] There were also numerous criticisms of Cardinal Migazzi, interspersed with scandalous anecdotes in the most dubious taste to keep up the interest of less intellectually inclined readers. The book was poorly received in intellectual circles because of its overall lack of clarity and cohesion and might well have led to Friedel's premature demise as an author, had it not been so sharply attacked by the clerical conservatives that the liberals felt themselves obliged to come to his defense.[39] This was very timely assistance, because Friedel, who held no job in the bureaucracy and had been trying to make a living with his pen, found that publishers, giving as an excuse that whatever they brought out would be pirated at once, paid very little. He had been trying to make ends meet by *Vielschreiberei*, making up in sheer volume for what quality would not provide him with, and his health had suffered as a result.[40]

Friedel's newly achieved notoriety enabled him to place a play with the Burgtheater.[41] *Christel und Gretchen* is anything but a masterpiece of the drama, but it did give Friedel the opportunity to air some relatively daring opinions on social questions. Christel, a peasant, having laid his father to rest, puts in a claim for a sum of money owed the deceased by the lord of the region. The steward turns him away indignantly, claiming that it was the dead father who had owed the lord twice the amount claimed by Christel. Some of the young rustic's friends now advise him to go to court, but he is not all that naive. He tells them that after he has distributed half his money in bribes to various functionaries of the court and spent the other half on lawyers he will, under the most favorable circumstances, be left with a ver-

38. Friedel, *Briefe aus Wien*, pp. 71–75.
39. Gugitz, "J. F. Friedel," pp. 226–227.
40. Becker, *Der deutsche Roman*, p. 36.
41. J. Friedel, *Christel und Gretchen: Eine ländliche Posse* (Vienna, 1785).

dict in his favor and nothing else.[42] Friedel, like Huber, is saying
that in spite of the judicial reforms, nothing has really changed
in the rural courts.

At this point in the play Christel receives a message from the
lord, Sommerthal, suggesting that if Christel's fiancée, Gretchen,
will come to share his bed for a night, he will pay the alleged
debt. This intelligence puts Christel in a philosophic mood. He
soliloquizes that what he is faced with is a very ancient evil: the
irresponsible nobleman has always seduced the poor peasant
girls of his district, sending them away afterward with a small
gift of money and, as likely as not, a child in their bellies.[43] Subsequently, for no evident reason having to do with the plot, Sommerthal is made to deliver an absurd speech to his assembled
peasants, in which he tells them that they are persons of no consequence and that only money, which they can never expect to
have in any quantity, leads to gaining the respect of this world.[44]

Returning from the realm of lofty abstraction to his more
mundane interest in Gretchen, Sommerthal threatens that if she
does not submit to him soon, he will see to it that Christel disappears into the army. This threat so angers the peasants that
there are murmurings of rebellion. Gretchen's father, attempting
to calm the stormy waters, delivers an admonitory speech to
Sommerthal. He is an old man and has seen many things, but he
has never seen a subject refuse to obey his lord because the latter
cherished and protected him. All the peasant revolts he has seen
in his lifetime, and there have been many, were the direct result
of oppression and expropriation.[45] A series of odd misunderstand-

42. *Ibid.*, pp. 11–13.
43. *Ibid.*, p. 20.
44. *Ibid.*, p. 33. This has a false ring on not one but two counts. Peasants
were supposed to make use of traditional self-debasing formulas when con-
versing with their lords without having to be reminded to do so by the august
persons themselves—such reminders, if necessary, were left to the estate agents.
And a provincial magnate would not in all likelihood have looked on money as
being more important than land, position, and, above all, titles and derivation.
45. *Ibid.*, p. 100. This may well have been a direct allusion to the terrible
peasant uprising of 1775 in Bohemia.

ings now follows, in the course of which Christel makes an attempt on Sommerthal's life, but shoots Gretchen's father instead, thinks he has killed him, and runs away. Matters are not put to rights until the appearance of Sommerthal's noble fiancée, who lectures him as one would a negligent schoolboy—"unbesonnener . . ."—and leads her penitent swain away to a life of eternal fidelity.

What Prince Esterházy, to whom Friedel dedicated the play, made of all this is unfortunately not known. It is also a mystery how it could have passed the censorship. Although Friedel makes an attempt to mitigate Sommerthal's guilt to some extent, by blaming his scandalous behavior on advice given him by his crooked agent, the repeated denunciations of the conduct of the aristocracy, the bringing up of the most sensitive subject of peasant rebellion, and above all the hint at the possibility of tyrannicide should have assured its rejection.

In the same year Friedel also published a pamphlet offering unsolicited but detailed advice to the directors of the newly established poorhouse in Vienna, and a fantasy dealing with the social consequences of the newest triumph of science, the hot-air balloon: men would spend their days being wafted about by gentle breezes, and governments would be taken over by women.[46] It is by no means clear what the thrust of this generally murky piece was meant to be. He followed it with a novel attacking the Jesuits, by this time hardly a burning issue, and then concentrated his efforts entirely on the theater. In 1788 he became the director of the rather unsuccessful Theater auf der Wieden, and attracted attention by distributing free tickets among the poor of the city and by having the streets leading up to his suburban theater lighted at his own expense. By this time he was in the advanced stages of tuberculosis, and he died in 1789.[47]

Johann Pezzl, who was born in Lower Bavaria in 1756, studied

46. Gugitz, "J. F. Friedel," pp. 235–236.
47. *Ibid.*, p. 245.

law in Salzburg from 1776 to 1780, moved to Zürich the next year, coming to Vienna only in 1784, and who wrote most of his social and political satires before settling in Austria, is such a late *Zugereister* that there is a question whether he should be included in a discussion of Austrian literati at all.[48] But because his books enjoyed such widespread popularity in Austria, and because for some years after 1784 he was a prominent member of Vienna's literary world, it seems appropriate to do so.

Pezzl's first effort, a garden-variety attack on monasticism, added nothing to the literature of that already overexplored subject, but made it desirable for him to quit Salzburg for the rather more tolerant climate of Zürich, where he wrote his most famous book, *Faustin*.[49] Obviously modeled on *Candide*, the work describes the travail of a young man of sensibility who is looking for genuine enlightenment and toleration. A Pangloss figure, Father Boniface, tries throughout the book to convince Faustin that they are living in a genuinely philosophical century and that reason is everywhere triumphant, but somehow everything they come across is a living contradiction of his theory. Neither in the Catholic nor in the Protestant countries of Europe is true religious toleration to be found. And there is not a trace of rational behavior to be seen anywhere. Finally they come to Salzburg. At this point Pezzl cannot resist engaging in a bit of heavy-handed humor, and describes that city as by far the most enlightened in the whole of southern Germany. The two wanderers have all but decided to settle there when they are told that even more interesting developments are taking place in Vienna.[50] The last

48. Wurzbach, *Biographisches Lexicon*, XXII, 160; G. Gugitz, "Johann Pezzl," *J.G.G.*, XVI (1906), 185. O'Brien (*Religious Toleration*, p. 64), who describes Pezzl as "another representative Austrian radical," is for that reason wide of the mark.

49. J. Pezzl, *Faustin oder das philosophische Jahrhundert* (3rd ed., Vienna, 1785). Cf. O'Brien, *Religious Toleration*, p. 64, and Gugitz, "Johann Pezzl," p. 185.

50. Pezzl, *Faustin*, pp. 327–328. The only discussion of Joseph's reforms on a comparable scale is to be found in the work of the itinerant literatus Carl Ignatz Geiger, the author of the utopian travel journal *Reise eines Erdbewohners in den Mars,* who twice came to Vienna in the vain hope of finding employment

chapter of *Faustin* is a detailed examination of the Josephinian reform program. If evidently written with an eye on what advantages it might gain its author in Vienna, it is nevertheless of considerable interest, being the most complete contemporary evaluation of Joseph's reforms by an outsider. Pezzl's emphasis here is heavily on those measures which he considered to be tantamount to the disestablishment of the Catholic church in Austria, but he also finds space to praise Joseph's educational and judicial reforms.

On the strength of *Faustin* Pezzl came to Vienna, confident that he would find both a sympathetic reception and remunerative employment. Initially only the former expectation was realized, and for some time Pezzl, like Friedel, was forced to support himself by the rapid production of pamphlets. But he did have another arrow in his quiver. Before coming to Austria he had written another book, which he now published in Germany. This was the *Marokanische Briefe*, in form an obvious imitation of the *Lettres Persanes*. In content this work was varied. The greater part of it was given over to a renewed attack on intolerance, both Catholic and Protestant. Only toward the end did Pezzl turn his attention to political subjects. At that point he attacked polycracy, the notorious German *Kleinstaaterei*. For every princeling to maintain a separate army and a court of his own required so much money that the peasant had to be stripped naked. As soon as Germany united under a single ruler, her economic problems would be solved, and in addition her strength would be such that no other state would ever again dare to take the field against her.[51] In general, the quarrels of princes were vain and apt to be unleashed over nugatory causes, but once under way, they depopulated entire countrysides. Only the cease-

---

there. Being forced to depart empty-handed, he concluded that true enlightenment could not be enforced by ordinances; a long step-by-step preparation was necessary to cancel prejudices inculcated in people since birth. See the appendix to the facsimile edition of Geiger's utopia by J. Hermand (Stuttgart, 1967), p. 20.

51. J. Pezzl, *Marokanische Briefe* (2nd ed., Frankfurt a. M., 1784), pp. 249–252.

less and disinterested activities of scholars had, by humanizing princes and their ministers, prevented society from being debased to an entirely bestial level by constant warfare.[52] Joseph, however, unmoved even by these assurances, continued to deny Pezzl the employment which he so evidently deserved.

At last in 1786 Pezzl's Masonic friends secured for him the desirable post of secretary and chief librarian to Prince Kaunitz.[53] Thereafter, perhaps because of his disappointment with Joseph's continuing reserve toward Masonry,[54] or because he became increasingly disenchanted with the Austrian enlightenment, which he had come to think of as more rhetorical than seriously meant,[55] but more probably because he thought it prudent to imitate his employer's growing disaffection from almost all of Joseph's policies, an attitude that Kaunitz did not hesitate to display openly, Pezzl refrained from any additional liberal statements. Indeed, a sequel to his *Moroccan Letters* that appeared in 1787 was highly critical of the excesses of the enlightenment and was permeated by a spirit of aristocratic detachment from the problems of the day that Pezzl had obviously copied from his employer but that rather ill suited him.[56]

No account of the circle of young Viennese poets would be complete without mention of Joseph Franz Ratschky. Born in Vienna in 1757, he took a job as a clerk in the imperial surveying department, later had himself transferred to the *Hofkanzlei*, where he was employed as a supervising official in the state lottery, and ended his administrative career most respectably as principal secretary to the president of the government of Upper Austria. In 1777, having established effective control over the intricacies of the lottery, he was able to take on the editorship of the *Wiener Musenalmanach*. Although he was forced to give

---

52. *Ibid.*, pp. 241–245.
53. Gugitz, "Johann Pezzl," p. 193.
54. *Ibid.*
55. Thus O'Brien, *Religious Toleration*, p. 65, who bases his case on a letter of Pezzl's to a friend in Zürich.
56. Gugitz, "Johann Pezzl," p. 195.

up that position three years later, he remained the friend and confidant of most of the members of the Viennese intelligentsia throughout the 1870's. His own publications in this period were limited to scattered poems without particular social or political content.[57]

Finally, Gottlieb Leon belonged to this circle. Born in Vienna in 1757, he eventually found employment in the imperial library. Although his own literary production was sparse, consisting of only occasional poetry, his friends believed that he possessed uncommonly developed critical faculties and frequently asked his opinion of their work. In 1787, in a letter to Reinhold, he passed a summary and entirely negative judgment on them all: "I doubt very much if Austrian literature will ever attain the level of a genuine culture. Writers and poets here are far more interested in pursuing their numberless feuds than in improving the quality of their work."[58] But perhaps he was embittered about his own work not being more highly regarded.

So far this account has concentrated on the literary world of Vienna to the almost entire exclusion of the provinces. This is not the result of big-city chauvinism or even of an unwitting parochialism which hears only the loudest voice, but a matter of practical necessity. Upon the accession of Joseph everyone who detected within himself even the vaguest promise that he might some day develop into a writer descended on the capital, so that, briefly at least, the Austrian pattern was modeled on the French one of concentration rather than on the more typically German one of cultural diffusion. Those who remained behind in the provinces had, almost without exception, good reasons for their diffidence. The work of the Benedictine abbot Anselm von Edling, who was regarded as one of the lights of the Carinthian enlightenment, may, not altogether unfairly, stand for them all.

---

57. Wurzbach, *Biographisches Lexicon*, XXV, 22–24; Nadler, *Literaturgeschichte*, pp. 194–198.

58. Leon to Reinhold, November 3, 1787, Keil, *Wiener Freunde*, p. 69; Wurzbach, *Biographisches Lexicon*, XV, 1. This negative judgment of Leon's is often quoted by those wishing to denigrate Austrian culture of the period.

In 1784 he published a poem, *Trial on Mount Olympus*, in which the gods, angry with Blumauer for having insulted them, put him on trial for his life. The verdict, of course, was a triumphant acquittal:

> So endigt sich der Götterrath
> Die Juno kriegt's Laxieren;
> Venus die es behauptet hat,
> Scheint ihr zu insultieren;
> Die Kläger steh'n versteinert da,
> Blumauer fährt in Gloria
> Nach seinem Wien herunter.[59]

Edling's monastery was dissolved in 1787, not nearly soon enough to have prevented the creation of this and similar monstrosities.

While the provinces contributed less than their share to the literature of Josephinism, a by no means negligible amount of it was produced outside of the boundaries of the Hapsburg monarchy. Many of the German *Aufklärer*, reacting to the fascinating news emanating from Vienna, decided that here was an opportunity made to order for them. Some of them were merely anxious to participate in what they mistakenly regarded as a forthcoming distribution of spoils; others availed themselves of the opportunity to pass judgment on what, at least initially, struck them as a rare enough phenomenon, the practical implementation of the very sort of philosophical system they had been writing about all along.

A genuinely disinterested commentator of the second type was the Swiss philosopher, educational reformer, and philosopher of history Isaak Iselin. From the time of Joseph's accession in 1780 until the time of his own death two years later, he filled the pages of a journal which he edited, the *Ephemeriden*, with detailed reports about the most recent reforms announced in Vienna. He supported the edicts of toleration with undisguised enthusiasm, and waxed eloquent about the merits of Joseph's reform of primary education. He was less happy about the

---

59. E. Nussbaumer, *Geistiges Kärnten* (Klagenfurt, 1956), pp. 228–235.

dissolution of the monasteries, but supported it as a sad but necessary step. He began to draw back, however, when he reached the conclusion that Joseph's anti-clerical policy was being implemented with a fanaticism that would have done honor to the most reactionary defenders of the church. And he rejected without qualification the hysterical tone that characterized many of the pamphlets coming out of Vienna, writing to a friend: "There is no need to heap insults upon throne and altar in order to be a friend of truth and a defender of humanity."[60] Had Iselin lived but a short time longer, he would very probably have turned completely away from Joseph.

This is what Christoph Martin Wieland, one of the most influential of the German *Aufklärer*, did, although for reasons that undoubtedly were less elevated than Iselin's insistence that even superstition had a right to exist. In mid-career, when he had achieved a comfortable position as a resident sage in the principality of Weimar, notorious for a climate favorable to the enlightenment, Wieland apparently decided that his no doubt considerable talents were worthy of an even more glittering showcase, and in consequence launched into a concerted effort to attract favorable attention in Vienna. Equipped with a fair amount of prescience, Wieland noticed as early as 1772 that the future belonged to Joseph, and that there was no better way to gain the Emperor's sympathetic attention than to attack the abuses characterizing the church. Accordingly, he wrote a utopia, *The Golden Mirror*, which, while it denounced a long list of abuses known to be inherent in the Austrian church, very carefully avoided any sign of an overt attack on the Catholic religion.[61] This was all to the good, but unfortunately for the success of his undertaking, Wieland did not stop there. Rather, he went on to comment at length on the political conditions which obtained in his ideal world. He began safely enough with

60. U. Im Hof, *Isaak Iselin und die Spätaufklärung* (Berne and Munich, 1967), pp. 196–197.
61. C. M. Wieland, *Der goldene Spiegel* (Leipzig, 1772).

the description of a duodecimo utopia strongly reminiscent of Weimar, which, as he hastened to flatter Joseph by pointing out, could only exist given the generosity and forbearance of its powerful neighbors. But, he wrote, it was also possible to achieve at least a working approximation of the ideal state on a large scale, and to this end he launched into a description of the country of Schechian, clearly meant to represent Austria.

In Schechian every citizen was, first of all, a servant of the state. The clergy was required to be at the service of the ruler no less than any other estate, and those priests who put their loyalty to the church above that due to the state were summarily expelled. In return, the state used the great resources concentrated in this manner in the most rational way imaginable. Soldiers, for instance, who had great blocks of free time at their disposal because Schechian was a peace-loving country, were regularly employed in helping the peasants bring in the harvest. The ruler, whose powers derived, somewhat redundantly, both from the Grace of God and from the social contract, was loved by all. So far as this went, it might still have achieved Wieland's ends, but he could not resist digging into the past history of Schechian. It seems that the political situation there had not always been so idyllic. As a matter of fact, the previous ruler had been a gross and notorious tyrant, and his wise and enlightened successor, to whom the country owed its happiness, had displaced him on the throne with the help of a popular uprising. Wieland rather lamely tried to mitigate the evil by the subsequent revelation that the good prince was, in reality, the legitimate heir to the throne, but the fact remained that he had ascended to it in an unmistakably illegal manner, and so far as Joseph was concerned, the harm was done. Wieland sent him an inscribed copy of the work accompanied by an effusive letter, but received no reply.[62]

Undismayed by this failure, Wieland redoubled his efforts.

62. F. Sengle, *Wieland* (Stuttgart, 1949), pp. 259–267.

He entered into a correspondence with Baron Gebler, whose exiguous dramas he praised even more extravagantly than Nicolai. In the pages of a journal which he founded shortly thereafter, the *Teutscher Merkur*, he dropped repeated hints to Joseph that he was missing a unique opportunity to gain immortal fame as a patron of literature, but all to no avail.[63] By 1780 he had given up hope. He entered into a long dispute with Friedrich Gottlieb Klopstock, who maintained that Joseph's recent accession to sole power would raise the curtain on an age in which the human spirit would at last triumph over darkness. Wieland argued that the highest form of human achievement, a society based on the unsurpassed canons of the classical world, was possible only in such isolated backwaters as Weimar, shielded as these were from the vulgar and debilitating hubbub of the great world. He refused to open the pages of his journal to the many panegyrists who now wished to praise Joseph in public, saying somewhat grandiloquently that if the Emperor chose to ignore his existence, he was perfectly capable of reciprocating in kind.[64] Wieland had done with Joseph.

Johann Ferdinand Gaum made up for his relative obscurity as a literary figure with a much greater persistence. Born in Württemberg in 1738, he became a Jesuit and for a time taught philosophy in a seminary. By 1778 he had broken with the church. Thus Joseph's accession saw him well prepared to join in the scramble for preferment that was now to attract participants from all over Germany. He wrote pamphlets on the Pope's visit to Vienna, on his subsequent inglorious return to Rome, on the evils of monasticism, on the need to abolish sacerdotal celibacy, on the decline of the Catholic hierarchy, and on the right of the state to legislate for the church.[65] None of this, however, resulted in particular notice being taken of him in Vienna,

63. *Ibid.*, pp. 268–272.
64. *Ibid.*, pp. 280, 385.
65. G. C. Hamberger, *Das gelehrte Teutschland* (24 vols., Lemgo, 1796–1834), XI, 257–259.

where such materials were not precisely in short supply. Gaum tried again some time later with a more ambitious work, a report of a conversation conducted in the realm of the dead between Maria Theresa and Frederick the Great, a literary form which had become very popular.[66] While this was quite evidently written to catch the market for Friedericiana that the Prussian king's death had created, it also kept in mind the additional possibility of currying some useful favor in Vienna. However, as Gaum could not resist giving Frederick almost all the good lines, it is hardly surprising that he failed to achieve much of an effect.

66. J. F. Gaum, *Gespräch im Reiche der Toten zwischen Maria Theresia und Friedrich dem Zweyten* (5 vols., Malta [Ulm], 1788–87).

6

The Paladins of Josephinism: The Radicals

IT WILL not have escaped the attentive reader's attention that even among the more moderate supporters of Joseph's reform program a certain disenchantment seems to have set in after 1785. Their support for his various reform measures became less vocal, and here and there a critical note crept in. There were several reasons for the developing alienation of the Emperor's supporters. First, as has already been noted, at the time of the six-ducat affair in 1784 strong pressures to tighten up the censorship became manifest. And although the six-ducat scheme was finally dropped, new instructions went out to the censors, ordering them not to pass "useless material, filled with nonsense or with attacks on good morals and the clergy." The period of almost unlimited freedom of expression was over and not a few writers now came to find this out to their disadvantage.[1]

Second, the depredations of the literary pirates, which up until this time had been chiefly harmful to the profits of foreign writers, were now beginning to affect the domestic literati. In November, 1784, the situation became critical. Trattner, who had concluded that at least some of the production of the local scribblers would repay reprinting, submitted a "Plan for the

1. Nagl, Zeidler, and Castle, *Literaturgeschichte*, II, 248–249; Sashegyi, *Zensur und Geistesfreiheit*, p. 84.

General Furtherance of Reading" to the government which proposed that, in the interest of the reading public, he would offer all Austrian writers the opportunity of signing exclusive agreements with him. If they refused, he would have no compunction about reprinting all their works. There was an immediate and anguished protest by practically all the leading Austrian writers, including Haschka, Sonnenfels, Denis, Blumauer, and Born. But Joseph, to whom the economies which the sort of centralization of all literary production that Trattner's scheme seemed to promise were irresistible, gave his blessing to the proposal. Not surprisingly, his popularity with the literati was not enhanced.[2]

Furthermore, all hopes of winning the Emperor over to a more active support of Free Masonry had by then been pretty well given up as chimerical. Joseph had steadfastly refused to be drawn into the movement, and his attitude toward it became noticeably more suspicious and negative. At last, toward the end of 1785, he issued a new regulation, the *Freimaurerpatent*, which severely restricted the Masons in their activities. Hereafter only one lodge was to be permitted in the capital city of each province; all others were to be dissolved and unsanctioned meetings were to be punished under the laws forbidding unallowed games of chance; and the lodges were required to submit membership lists to the police and to keep these up to date quarterly.[3] Some of the literati, like Born, chose to follow the Emperor's strong hint and severed their connections with the Masons, but the majority did not and bore Joseph a grudge.

Last, it should be taken into consideration that by 1785 Joseph's political honeymoon was well over. His measures had had five years to produce results. Of necessity, they had not done so in all cases, and there were many who had become dissatisfied merely on this ground.

To be sure, there were those who may even at the outset not have been convinced utterly that the best method to govern in

2. Goldfriedrich, *Deutschen Buchhandels*, p. 81.
3. Gräffer, *Josephinische Curiosa*, I, 42–45.

the interest of the greatest number was to resort to enlightened despotism. One of these potential malcontents was Heinrich Gottfried Brettschneider. Born in Gera, in the district of Wettin, in 1739, he took service in a Saxon cavalry regiment, served with distinction in the Seven Years' War, was commissioned after the battle of Kolin, transferred to the Prussian service, was captured by the French, and upon his release after the end of hostilities was promoted to major. In 1772 he left the service and traveled for a year in France, the Netherlands, and England. In the mid-1770's he came to Vienna and obtained a subsidiary government job through the good offices of Baron Gebler, who subsequently introduced him into Viennese Masonic circles. Brettschneider also had entrée to the houses of the leading Viennese Jews, including the Arnstein family.[4] His new post, however, being in the provincial administration of the Banat, soon took him away from Vienna. In 1780 he was promoted and transferred to Budapest. There he found himself surrounded by anti-Josephinian reactionaries, with whom he engaged in ceaseless polemics. These gained him the reputation of being the only liberal in a desert of Magyar conservatism, and Joseph for a time considered whether it would not be useful to bring him to Vienna, where his sphere of action would be much expanded. But he was dissuaded from doing so because Brettschneider had compromised himself to a fatal extent by his actions at the time of Nicolai's visit to Vienna in 1781. It was widely and probably accurately believed that most of the derogatory information about persons in Vienna which Nicolai had published in his *Reisebeschreibung* had been supplied by Brettschneider, who had a low opinion of the Viennese intelligentsia. As a result, in 1782 Brettschneider was transferred instead to Lemberg, a post which he disliked intensely.[5]

Brettschneider had made his debut as a writer as early as

4. Wurzbach, *Biographisches Lexicon*, II, 140–143; Nagl, Zeidler, and Castle, *Literaturgeschichte*, II, 408; K. Emmerich, *Der Wolf und das Pferd: Deutsche Tierfabeln des 18. Jahrhunderts* (Berlin, 1960), p. 282.
5. *Ibid.*

1768 with a satirical poem entitled *Graf Esau* that made fun of the extravagant life-style that prevailed among diplomats. In 1774, immediately following upon his arrival in Vienna, he published a pamphlet, evidently the result of his observations made during his travels in western Europe, which came as close to arguing for deism as it was possible to do in the Austria of that day.[6] Now, in the midst of quarreling with his Hungarian colleagues in Budapest, he took to writing animal fables, a form of political commentary that had long been popular both in France and Germany, but which unaccountably had found no practitioners in Austria.[7] Most of these fables were both politically innocuous and traditional in their form, as for instance *Die Heirat des Esels*: an ass, no longer content with his position in society, is advised by his friends that the best way to rise in the world is to marry above his station. He finds an old mare who consents to become his wife. In no time at all she is leading him a merry chase and he realizes, too late, that by intruding where he was not wanted he has only succeeded in making a fool of himself.

Very different, however, is the fable *Der Reichstag der Spatzen*. The sparrows, appalled that of late men have been shooting them on sight, deliberate about the reasons for their evident unpopularity. The consensus is that their singing voices are displeasing to human ears, and that they would do well to pray to God to give them more pleasing ones. But at the last moment one gray old bird objects:

> Die Zunge ist's—die Stimme nicht,
> Warum der Mensch uns sucht zu töten.
>
> Die Fressbegierde geht zu weit,
> Ihr wisst nichts von Genügsamkeit,
> Drum will man euch die Kost verteurn.
> Ihr sucht das beste Korn mit Fleiss

6. H. G. v. Brettschneider, *Die Religion mit philosophischen Augen betrachtet* (Vienna, 1774).

7. H. G. v. Brettschneider, *Fabeln, Romanzen und Sinngedichte* (Frankfurt a. M. and Leipzig, 1781).

> Und stehlt des Landsmanns sauern Schweiss
> Vom Ackerfeld und aus den Scheuern.

> Drum, Brüder, wollt ihr sicher sein,
> So stellt das schnöde Naschen ein
> Und lernt ein wenig mässig leben.

The rest of the sparrows cavil at being told such home truths:

> Er will wir sollen mässig sein,
> das geht kein edler Sperling ein.

They fall upon him, tear him to pieces, and fly off in search of a voice instructor. Thereupon the moral is drawn:

> Dies Schicksal schrecke niemand ab,
> Und wem der Himmel Gaben gab,
> Der dien dem Staate, nicht dem Magen.
> Wer Armer Schweiss sein Erbrecht nennt,
> Brot stiehlt, dass er verdienen könnt,
> Den soll man aus dem Lande jagen.

The exploiters of the peasants, the aristocrats, have failed to draw the obvious lesson from previous peasant rebellions. Let them therefore be chased out of the country. In contrast to similar and contemporary fables written in Germany, the tone is not one of moral indignation—the world is evil, would that God were pleased to change it—but of social outrage. Unlike similar German attacks on duodecimo absolutism, there is no appeal to a higher instance in the form of the Emperor to set matters right. Rather, the peasants are encouraged to resort to self-help in order to rid themselves of their oppressors.[8]

One fable does not a revolution make, but the language of the *Reichstag der Spatzen* is just barely within the bounds of language that could be used by a loyal servant of the crown without running the gravest risk of being deprived of position and liberty. One wonders whether Joseph had read it when he proposed to further Brettschneider's career. Or perhaps he thought with Sonnenfels that the peasants, in fact, did not do much read-

8. Cf. Emmerich, *Wolf und Pferd*, pp. 7–15.

ing. As for Brettschneider, his revolutionary ardor seems to have subsided in the long years he spent as chief librarian at the University of Lemberg. He did publish some relatively mild sorties against the religious establishment, and an attack on secret societies that corresponded so closely with Joseph's opinion of the Masons that he was thereafter repeatedly commissioned to write official pamphlets for the government. Many years later he produced a call for national union against the French invaders, *Theodor*.[9] His radical period had, it would seem, been very brief, but for all that, it was unmistakable.

Like Brettschneider, Wilhelm Friedrich von Mayern had been a soldier. Born in Anspach in 1760, he grew up to study law at Altdorf and Erlangen. Influenced by a rather too massive dose of travel literature that he had ingested as a youth, he made plans to emigrate to America. When this plan proved impossible of realization because of a lack of means, he did the next best thing: he joined the Austrian artillery, in which he had somehow managed to wangle a commission. While on garrison duty he made the acquaintance of two young noblemen who were on the Grand Tour. A firm friendship was soon formed, and Mayern resigned his commission to accompany the travelers in a capacity that seems to have struck a balance between that of companion and of factotum. They traveled to England, Scotland, back through Germany to Poland, Hungary, Italy, Greece, and Asia Minor. Everywhere classical sites were sought out and "done" with fanatical zeal. On the way back Mayern's friends either grew tired of his company, or there may have been a quarrel; at any rate he was left behind in Sicily, where for some time he was stranded without funds. Having experienced a surfeit of ruins, he spent the period of his enforced stay in close observation of local conditions. He eventually made his way to Rome, whence with the help of the Austrian embassy he returned to his adopted homeland. After a time he succeeded in regaining his commis-

9. Nagl, Zeidler, and Castle, *Literaturgeschichte*, II, 408.

sion and, perhaps with the help of Prince Schwarzenberg, who had befriended him, obtained the most sought-after duty in the army, a permanent assignment in Vienna.[10] There, although there is no evidence that would suggest that he had any contacts with the literary world, he occupied himself with the composition of a novel. For reasons that will presently become clear, he submitted it to the censorship as a translation from the Sanskrit, but in spite of the prevailing rage for exotica the censor refused to pass it. Thus Mayern was obliged to publish his book abroad in 1787.[11]

Dya-Na-Sore is not an easy book to summarize. It suffers at the same time from being the quintessence of the novel in letter form, with letters within letters and whole journals within those, and from being unmistakably an anticipation of a breathless romantic exaltation. Apart from its utter formlessness, it is also marked by an insufferable preachiness, longueurs that are anything but divine, and a massive degree of ideological confusion. Nevertheless, this unappetizing mixture contains some remarkable notions. To give as succinct as possible an account of the plot of the work, a young man of apparently exquisite sensitivity goes to India in search of a new and more perfect society. In a series of letters written in Benares he reports to a friend on how his quest has fared. He himself has failed to find any evidence of the higher values that he had been led to believe were nurtured in the East, but he has met another young European, a certain W., whose interests are similar to his and who, more adventurous still, had struck out in the direction of faraway Tibet. Poor W. comes to grief when his horse carries him over the side of a cliff,

10. Wurzbach, *Biographisches Lexicon*, XVII, 179–185; E. J. Görlich, *Einführung in die Geschichte der österreichischen Literatur* (Vienna, 1946), p. 72.

11. W. F. v. Mayern, *Dya-Na-Sore* (5 vols., Frankfurt a. M., 1787). There is an abridged version of the work in J. Kürschner, *Deutsche National-Literatur* (163 vols., Berlin, 1884–93), CXXXVII. Kürschner introduces the book, which he dismisses somewhat airily as having no literary merit whatever, with an angry denunciation of fuzzy-minded idealists who would have done much better to concern themselves with subjects more in keeping with their stations in life.

but his body is recovered. Letters and a journal found on his person are brought to the narrator in Benares.

Essentially two separate stories are contained in these. The first concerns W.'s adventures at the court of the Dalai Lama. What strikes him as most remarkable is that people from the farthest corners of Asia make their way there in search of advice and comfort. They have been brought to Lhassa by the assurances of the great man's disciples, who claim that he has the gift of seeing straight into a man's heart. Nothing is further from the truth: the Lama is only a puppet who is manipulated at will by his servants. A religion, born out of a once-felt need for purity and truth, has been corrupted and turned into a profit-making venture by scoundrels. Far better that no great man should ever live, than to have his work debased by eternally avaricious hordes of self-seeking disciples. Considerations on this order lead to the appointment of a governmental commission to investigate the lamasery. It reports that a scandalous shallowness pervades all aspects of its life: at best the doctrines it teaches are based on unproven assumptions no better than probabilism; at worst they are outright lies.[12] As a deistic attack on the religious establishment, complete with an obsequious appeal to the secular authority as the only possible restorer of truth and light, this was in no way either new, or different from what Mayern could have read in the course of the last seven years in every coffee house in Vienna. But there was more to come.

In W.'s recovered journal there is a lengthy account of a scene which he witnessed in the course of his travels. A father, who had been offended in some way by a neighboring tribesman, sends his three sons on an expedition to avenge him. Before their ultimate departure there is a leave-taking of such inordinate—even stupendous—length that the reader is reduced to pleading for a change of heart on the part of the father, which at least would put an end to the scene. All to no avail: Mayern is relent-

12. Mayern, *Dya-Na-Sore*, Kürschner ed., pp. 390–391.

less. In the course of this never-ending scene, the father proffers advice to each of his sons, which by comparison turns Polonius into a profound and original thinker. But at last the old man's mood changes and he addresses himself to particulars. These, it turns out, are neither banal nor shopworn. He now tells his sons that not only the church but the state as well must always be treated with the greatest suspicion. In almost every land one can find a small man who, trading on the need of the mass of people to treat someone with adulation, has been made to seem great. Only the really wise man can summon enough detachment to laugh at him and at his incense-burning devotees.[13] How has it come to this?, for once men were free. It seems that almost from the beginning tyrants lurked about, waiting for their opportunity to enslave men. Making use chiefly of the wiles of women, they corrupted the mass of little men, who in their innocence surrendered their rights in exchange for transient pleasures and evanescent luxuries.[14] If one had not read something very like this in Rousseau, one would at this point begin to harbor doubts about Mayern's sanity.

But what most arouses the old man's indignation is that in order to fill their always-empty stomachs, men are forever rushing voluntarily into slavery. In the best-run state, merely let someone appear who proposes to transform the bonds of the law into the chains of slavery, and thousands will rush to him begging to be enslaved. Men are not only unhappy, but they are themselves responsible for their unhappiness. There is nothing to be done, it is the way of the world; for the wise man complete indifference to his surroundings is the only possible consolation.[15] The noblest of the three sons, Dya, will have nothing to do with such counsels of despair. People, he maintains, must be educated to give their loyalties to the state and not to a tyrant, must be steeped in history so that they will instantly recognize the many

13. *Ibid.*, p. 406.
14. *Ibid.*, p. 417.
15. *Ibid.*, pp. 419–420.

possible forms that subversion of justice takes. Religion too must serve the higher interest, that of the state. The army must not be an extension of the monarch's will, but should be made up of representatives of all the people, the final and highest expression of the people's will. In order for all this to happen, it is above all necessary for every man to be strong, for only real men can survive in the proximity of kings.[16]

Later, a story about a faraway land with a young and likely-looking ruler is told. With the best of intentions, he attempts to change some of the more outmoded customs of his country. Inevitably he meets with resistance from those whose traditional privileges he is infringing. Over the long run this so infuriates him that he abandons all moderation, forces more and more outlandish reforms down the unwilling throats of his subjects, and finishes by oppressing them no less than the most ruthless of tyrants. The moral is plain: no single man can be expected to know what the mass of men desire. This much *Menschenkenntniss* must not be looked for in a mere mortal.[17]

It takes no miracles of perception to recognize the outline of Joseph's portrait in these lines. But we have here no mere remonstrance, not just a criticism of Joseph for unduly hastening the pace. If this was not an expression of republican sentiments, it at least came uncomfortably close. Certainly it by far exceeded anything that might reasonably be subsumed under the rubric of advice to princes. Still later, Mayern goes well beyond merely despairing of the abilities of enlightened despotism to alter the completely unsatisfactory state of human affairs. Ultimately, at least on the local level, the evil is inherent in the situation of Germany. No state which does not have a seacoast can ever be really free. A continental people will forever and necessarily dissipate its energies in narrowly conceived and meaningless quarrels with its neighbors. It has no horizon, no possibility of escape into the infinite space to which the sea gives access. The

16. *Ibid.*, pp. 420–425; Görlich, *Einführung*, p. 72.
17. Mayern, *Dya-Na-Sore*, IV, 65–69.

eternally landlocked can never expect to be anything but slaves.[18]

In spite of all this, apart from being refused permission to publish his book in Austria, Mayern seems to have suffered no ill effects as the result of his massive effrontery. Although he did not again try his hand at writing, he had a long if somewhat undistinguished career in the army, which was crowned with a respectable staff appointment after the Napoleonic Wars.

The career of Franz Kratter was rather more conventional. Born in Swabia in 1758, he attended a Jesuit school in Augsburg from which he was ultimately expelled, and came to Vienna in 1779 to study law. At Joseph's accession he hurried to join the horde of job-hunters who hoped to find positions consonant with their intellectual achievements in the reign of the new prince of humanists. Unlike most of these would-be placemen, Kratter actually found employment, becoming secretary to Prince Liechtenstein. But having cleared the first hurdle, he found that his literary talents were not sufficient to gain for him a recognized place in the world of Viennese belles lettres, whose standards at the time, it must be added, were not inordinately high. Thus Kratter's literary production of the 1780's must be viewed in the first instance as a repeated attempt to gain the entrée that had been denied him, the work of an outsider seeking to call attention to himself.[19]

In 1781 Kratter tried his luck with a poem about the Augarten, a favorite subject of writers wanting to flatter Joseph as a great humanitarian for having opened that park, hitherto the exclusive preserve of the court and the high nobility, to the public. But since the poem was as lacking in ideas as it was deficient in meter, it brought him no recognition.[20] Almost three years later, he tried again with a short novel, *Der junge Mahler am*

---

18. *Ibid.*, V, 184–185. There are, of course, unmistakable echoes of Montesquieu here.

19. Wurzbach, *Biographisches Lexicon*, XIII, 144; G. Gugitz, "Franz Kratter," *J.G.G.*, XXIV (1913), 242–246.

20. Gugitz, "Franz Kratter," p. 247.

Hofe, in which a mindless and static plot was not in any material way improved upon by an occasional attempt to popularize the Josephinian reform program on the most banal possible level.[21] By this time, although still denied full membership in the Viennese society of poets, he had risen sufficiently high in the world to be welcomed as a Mason. Shortly thereafter, he took a long journey through Galicia, in part for family reasons, but also, it seems, in the hope of being appointed to a chair at the new university in Lemberg. In this expectation he was disappointed, and finally was forced to return to Vienna empty-handed. His visit to Poland, however, provided him with the material both for taking revenge on those who had failed to reward him according to his true merits and for bringing himself once again to the attention of the Emperor.

Galicia, which had been notoriously misgoverned even by Polish standards, had proven too hard a nut to crack for the Austrian officials sent there after the First Partition in 1772. The corruption, neglect, and inefficiency which still prevailed at all levels of life presented an inviting target to the would-be social critic. Kratter now published a report about what he had observed in the course of his journey.[22] Because this was so manifestly meant to advance his career in Austria, it cannot quite be taken at face value as an accurate description of Galician conditions. To make up for this, it provides valuable insights into what sort of arguments he regarded as suited to the accomplishment of his end. Even so, Kratter's enthusiasms eventually run away with him, and he finishes by arguing points that were close to his heart and could not conceivably have inspired confidence in Joseph.

Kratter's book aroused such indignation in Lemberg that

21. *Ibid.,* p. 248.

22. F. Kratter, *Briefe über den itzigen Zustand von Galizien* (2 vols., Leipzig, 1786). Throughout Kratter attributes the misery of the Galician peasant to the rapaciousness of the nobleman, abetted by that of the Jewish tavern-keeper. The former must be curbed, the latter turned to economically less damaging pursuits. See, for instance, I, 172ff., and II, 38ff.

when a group of irate citizens hung a copy of it from the gallows, no one could be found to take it down and the public hangman had to be hired at considerable expense to perform this function. It also failed to achieve its desired effect in Vienna. In fact, Kratter was expelled from the Masons shortly after its appearance.[23] By now thoroughly disabused of the notion that someday he might achieve preferment, he spent the next year in traveling. He traversed most of southern Germany and then, judging that the storm had quieted, returned to Galicia, where he published the journal which he had kept during his trip. As he had given up hope of ever getting a government job, he did not hesitate to speak his mind on a number of subjects. Of particular interest is his critique of the judicial system as it touches upon the lives of ordinary men. He argues that in all criminal cases the defendant, even if completely without means, should be represented by a competent attorney; and that it is not enough merely to punish a man with a term of imprisonment: the state must take some responsibility for what happens to him after his release from jail, lest he slide back into a life of crime.

In another series of essays Kratter addresses himself to the military establishment of the Habsburg monarchy. It is, he says, not only inefficient, but attracts the worst sort of low-life types. He concludes that the only practical method of doing away with the odium that has become attached to the military estate and to make it again possible for a respectable man to consider a military career is to resort to universal conscription.[24] It should not come as a surprise to anyone that this work was turned down by the Austrian censors.

In this period Kratter also wrote a novel whose heroine, a master cutler's daughter, maintains her virtue in spite of all the snares put in her path by gentlemen of quality, particularly by those of the cloth. Scenes depicting, in loving detail, narrowly

23. Gugitz, "Franz Kratter," p. 252.
24. *Ibid.*, pp. 259–260.

averted rapes in vestries and parish houses are interspersed with laboriously reasoned arguments against auricular confession and denunciations of the intolerant spirit of the clergy.[25] The conclusion that lasciviousness goes hand in hand with doctrinal rigidity and adherence to old forms seems inescapable.

Kratter had for years tried to be taken on in the bureaucracy without any success, and now that he had given up hope and thrown caution to the winds, he suddenly saw his long quest rewarded. In 1790 he was offered a post in Lemberg. It was perhaps not all that he might have dreamed of. Not to put too fine a point on it, he became a government inspector in a plant processing kosher meat. In later years he was to complain frequently that his position did not reflect his true abilities, but it did supply him with the economic base to pursue a new career. He now became a prolific writer of farces for the German theater in Lemberg, a much safer occupation than that of political journalist in Franciscan Austria. It may well be argued that there had all along been some question about the depth of feeling that Kratter's more violent effusions drew upon. Perhaps they were really nothing more than the carping of the disappointed office-seeker who merely hopes to be bribed to desist from his outrageous behavior. But without any reasonable question, they place him well outside the ranks of those whose voices were never raised except in praise of Joseph's achievements.

The Hungarian Ignatius Aurelius Fessler, born in 1756 in Zurány, grew up wanting to become, presumably in order, a doctor and teacher of the church, a martyr, and a saint. To this end he applied for admission to the Jesuits in 1772, but was turned down because of his age, thus escaping the trauma of the dissolution. Instead he became a Capuchin. The strict discipline and austerity of this most ascetic branch of the Franciscans apparently did not strike him as a reasonable preparation for

25. F. Kratter, *Das Schleifermädchen aus Schwaben* (2 vols., Frankfurt a. M., 1790).

achievement of his goals, and he was soon threatening to leave the order. In order to dissuade him from carrying out that threat, his novice-master resorted to the rather extreme measure of encouraging him to read the works of Seneca. The thought of the great Stoic did not have the intended effect on young Fessler. Instead of resigning himself to his rather unattractive place in life, he developed a consuming passion for the reading of secular philosophy which threatened seriously to call into question the achievement of the goals he had set for himself. In quest of more knowledge than was available to him in the theology classes of his monastery, he blundered upon a group of Hungarian Jansenists gathered around the person of Count Joseph von Podmaniczky. The literature he was given to read there in short order brought about the complete collapse of his religious faith. He now spent his nights reading philosophy, literature, law, economics, and learning languages. His position appeared to him as entirely false; life in the monastery had become completely insupportable for him. He tried repeatedly but without success to secure a position as house chaplain, a situation that would have allowed him to pursue his various bents unhindered by the constraints of monastic life. It was in this frame of mind that in 1777 he was transferred to a house of his order located in the village of Schwechat, just outside of Vienna.[26]

In Schwechat, making use of his Hungarian connections, he soon established contact with the Viennese Jansenists, notably with Eybel and Rautenstrauch. Under the influence of these men he settled upon a minimal deism as the sole remnant of his commitment to religion and took an interest in the various schemes for social reform that were then being discussed in those circles. To pursue these interests further he arranged for a renewed transfer in 1781, this time to Vienna, and applied for permission to attend lectures at the university. But as his superiors in his new house did not deem it fitting for a monk to

26. Wurzbach, *Biographisches Lexicon*, IV, 201–204; P. F. Barton, "Ignatius Aurelius Fessler," *Kirche im Osten*, VII (1964), 110.

attend lectures in subjects aside from theology, he was turned down in this request.[27]

It was thus that a sullen and rebellious Fessler was suddenly called upon to perform a curious duty in February of 1782. A Hungarian monk was dying and, a rapid search having been conducted, it appeared that Fessler was the only member of his order within easy reach who spoke that language. Therefore he was taken to the Franciscan church on the Neuer Markt to hear his countryman's confession, and to his considerable surprise was led into a dungeon, below the level of even the imperial crypt, to a barred cell. Upon his inquiring, he was told that the wretch now breathing his last in these circumstances had been imprisoned in the same cell for the last fifty-two years. Now, all other considerations apart, monastic prisons had been abolished for all time by an imperial decree of 1771. As soon as the doors of the church had closed behind him, Fessler hurried to the nearby Hofburg to report the matter to Joseph himself. The ensuing investigation brought to light incredible conditions in numerous illegal monastery dungeons, resurrected many poor wretches who had not seen the light of day for decades, was directly responsible for the punitive dissolution of several monasteries, and did nothing to enhance Fessler's standing with his superiors in the order.[28]

His position was undermined further when he published a pamphlet attempting to demonstrate on the basis of arguments drawn from scripture and from the fathers of the church that secular authority had always taken precedence over ecclesiastical.[29] Shortly thereafter, due to the intervention of Baron Franz Karl Kressel, the president of Joseph's new Commission on Ecclesiastical Affairs, Fessler was at last granted permission to pursue his studies at the university. Apart from learning a number of ancient Oriental languages, he attended the lectures of

27. Barton, "I. A. Fessler," p. 111.
28. Lennhoff, *Die Freimaurer*, p. 166; Barton, "I. A. Fessler," p. 112.
29. I. A. Fessler, *Was ist der Kaiser?* (Vienna, 1782).

the celebrated Old Testament scholar Joseph Julian Monsper-
ger. The old man was put off by Fessler's obvious Jansenism, not
to say irreligiosity, but was much impressed by his linguistic accomplishments. In 1784, when a competition for a chair of
Oriental languages at the University of Lemberg was announced,
he encouraged Fessler to enter his name. Fessler's candidacy was
successful, in part because alone among all applicants he could
claim a knowledge of Syriac and Arabic, and also because Joseph,
remembering the affair of the dungeons, thought it fitting to
reward him.[30]

In Lemberg Fessler became a Mason while still remaining
a Capuchin. For a time he concentrated his energies on strictly
academic pursuits, hoping to establish himself as a sufficiently
eminent scholar to accomplish his transfer to a more important
and desirable post. But the economy-minded Joseph having reduced the number of Austrian universities, academic chairs were
at a premium. When after three years Fessler was still stuck in
Lemberg, his enthusiasm for Joseph and his works had diminished considerably. He now convinced himself that the Emperor's notorious harshness in reviewing judicial sentences was
proof that he was after all nothing but a tyrant. At the same
time a reading of Spinoza robbed him of the last vestige of any
commitment to formal religion.[31] It was thus in a very different
mood that he addressed himself once more to a wider public. In
1788 he wrote the historical drama *Sidney*, which was performed
on the Lemberg stage in the same year. A formless mishmash of
styles, alternating scenes of rape and barbarous executions in
Stuart England with prosy and declamatory speeches, it nevertheless contained a series of attacks on the tyrant James II which
imputed to him shortcomings that were recognizably those of
Joseph II. The play was closed down after one performance and
Fessler was accused of *lèse-majesté*. Deciding that at this point in

30. Boos, *Freimaurerei*, p. 387; Barton, "I. A. Fessler," p. 113.
31. Barton, "I. A. Fessler," p. 114.

his life martyrdom would no longer be consonant with his revised career goals, he escaped to Prussian Breslau.[32]

Before this precipitate end to his Austrian career, Fessler had been at work on what he intended to be his major statement on the great issues of the day. This was a strange combination of play, historical essay, and novel, dealing with the life of the Roman Emperor Marcus Aurelius, a work that was not published until after his flight from Austria.[33] Buried underneath an all but impenetrable mass of classical scholarship, and distributed over four thick volumes, there is a political message. Fessler has become disenchanted not only with Joseph, but with the principle of enlightened despotism, disputing the proposition that a ruler, no matter how well-intentioned, can ever discern what the real needs of the mass of his people are. Only a constitutionally limited monarch can be trusted over the long run not to abuse the power inherent in his position. Radical as this message may have been, it is highly unlikely that it could have reached any but the tiniest of audiences in the form in which it had been couched. Academicians had still to learn that if they wished to influence anyone aside from, possibly, their colleagues, they would have to put a curb on their deplorable tendency to display the full panoply of their learning on all possible and impossible occasions. Unfortunately Fessler's subsequent career, which saw him rise to become a bishop of the Lutheran church in Russia, is, in spite of its fascinating aspects, too far removed from our purview to consider here.

32. Nagl, Zeidler, and Castle, *Literaturgeschichte*, II, 410; Boos, *Freimaurerei*, p. 387; Barton, "I. A. Fessler," p. 118.
33. I. A. Fessler, *Marc-Aurel* (4 vols., 2nd ed., Breslau, 1793).

7

The Complete Josephinian: Joseph Richter

I F A man in the course of his life changes his opinions on the great questions too often, can always be depended on to sail before the wind, serves a new ideology with the same commitment that he had mustered for the old, the suspicion is close at hand that his enthusiasms are not all entirely genuine, that he is in fact an opportunist. Joseph Richter's career, spanning four reigns, always adapting itself, it seemed, to prevailing circumstances, has traditionally been viewed in such a light. Richter began as a minor lyricist rather in the tradition of the Jesuit bards, earned his spurs as an anti-clerical polemicist, became one of the leading propagandists for the Josephinian reforms, emerged as a critic of Joseph's lack of restraint while others were still celebrating his accomplishments, sang the praises of the wise policies of Leopold II, and ended as a semi-official spokesman of the Franciscan reaction. It is small wonder that he has been called "the voice of the semi-educated, smug Viennese petty bourgeoisie,"[1] the representative of a notorious *Spiessbürgerthum* whose interest in the concerns of the mind did not go beyond the point at which they could be dismissed with a few stale jokes in impatient anticipation of a copious and indeed excessive meal.

Yet to dismiss Richter in these terms is to miss the mark com-

1. Nagl, Zeidler, and Castle, *Literaturgeschichte*, II, 296.

pletely. Whatever weaknesses of character or lapses in constancy he may have been guilty of over the long run, for about fifteen years, from 1777 to 1792, he was without doubt the most perceptive and trenchant of all Austrian social critics. It would be committing a vulgar mistake to assume that because his ideas were presented in a comic and often deliberately grotesque form, they need not be taken seriously. In fact, they have a particular importance because they constitute a halfway house between the liberal position, the conviction that reform was necessary but that it could be achieved only with the traditional authority of the monarch, and radicalism, in this context the desire to enhance the value of proposed reforms by establishing constitutional guarantees that would prevent a future ruler from abrogating them at will.

Richter's origins are obscure. He was born in Vienna, sometime between 1740 and 1749, into a family that may just possibly have aspired to bourgeois status. As he grew up the family fortunes seem to have prospered, and he was able to matriculate in the faculty of philosophy in the University of Vienna. He does not seem to have kept at his studies for very long; the next thing that is known about him is that he worked in a subordinate capacity in a Viennese bank. By 1773 he was publishing occasional poems and writing intermittently for the *Musenalmanach*.[2] Having established himself as a published writer, like so many of his contemporaries he turned to the composition of plays for the Burgtheater, which since the de-emphasis of foreign works and the banning of the traditional *Hanswurst* had to be stoked with vast quantities of German dramas. Several of his plays passed across the boards there, and one of them that has survived, *The Creditor*, performed in 1777, is deserving of passing notice.[3]

A banker, Blum, is experiencing difficulties with defaulting

2. *Ibid.*, pp. 292–295. Wurzbach, *Biographisches Lexicon*, XXVI, 57–59, makes rather a hash of the account of Richter's life. See also W. Zitzenbacher, *Joseph Richter, bekannt als Eipeldauer* (Graz and Vienna, 1957), pp. 14–20.

3. J. Richter, *Der Gläubiger* (Vienna, 1773).

debtors. He thinks of going to court, but his bookkeeper, Ost, points out that in two recent bankruptcies in which a settlement had been reached by private agreement they had lost no more than 10 percent, while in another that had gone *ad cridam* they had recovered no more than one penny on the florin. Hungry ravens had appeared from all sides to tear off the piece of meat which, according to the dictates of custom, was theirs.[4] Ost, evidently an unquiet spirit, also complains that their aristocratic debtors treat Blum with marks of respect so long as they have his money in pocket, but as soon as the question of repayment arises he becomes nothing but a usurer and a Jew to them.[5] In the next scene Blum warns his daughter against taking the attentions of the young aristocrats who pay court to her too seriously. Unfortunately, what they really admire is not her beauty but his money.[6] Blum's factor, the Jew David, engages Ost in conversation. The bookkeeper laments that money cannot be taken into the other world, and that therefore, in a sense, all of his labors at the bank are in vain. David replies that the real pity is that one never has enough money in this world.[7] Throughout the rest of the play, which degenerates into a lightweight farce, the Jew is made to appear by far the most sensible and sympathetic character. Criticism of the court system, derogatory remarks about the nobility, and the introduction of likeable Jewish principals were, considering the period, an indication that Richter was willing to take at least some risks on behalf of his opinions.

In 1779 Richter made a trip to Paris, and another in 1782. His literary production for these years is sparse, and not much is known about how he occupied himself in this period. He did publish a pamphlet reporting the observations he had made in the course of his first journey. This was full of admiration for a great many aspects of French life and praised Joseph for attempt-

4. *Ibid.*, p. 6.
5. *Ibid.*, p. 10.
6. *Ibid.*, p. 28.
7. *Ibid.*, p. 44.

ing to reform Austria on the French model.[8] Upon his return from the second trip, however, works of all sorts began to flow from his pen at a genuinely impressive rate. The first of these, appearing in 1782, was a sort of philosophical dictionary, aimed at the man in the coffee house.[9] Its purpose was to disseminate the Josephinian *Aufklärung*, and its most frequent targets were monks, the church hierarchy, the still-persisting Viennese passion for aping foreign manners and institutions, the immorality of the ladies of Vienna, and the shortcomings of its writers. Interspersed among this was a leavening of social and occasionally even political criticism. Rather than to attempt to peel this out of its surroundings and group it artificially by subject matter, it seems preferable, in order not to lose the flavor entirely, to follow Richter's method, allowing oneself to be guided by the vagaries of the alphabet:

Allmosen. The truly needy man says: return to him at least part of the property which the more fortunate, or their ancestors, have deprived him of, be it through force or guile, and to which, as a human being and in accordance with natural law, he has as much right as they.[10]

Aufmunterung. For the German-speaking scholar it must be a sufficiency of encouragement not to be thrown in jail every time he dares to write something that is generally useful.[11]

Audienz. It seems that in a certain Oriental country the ruler customarily sleeps while granting audiences to his subjects; it is reliably reported that the result is the same as in many European lands where the prince listens to petitioners in a waking state.[12]

Blut. It is alleged that there are fundamental differences between noble and common blood; the only one that has so far been confirmed is that the latter is considerably healthier.[13]

---

8. J. Richter, *Reise von Wien nach Paris* (Vienna, 1781).
9. J. Richter, *A. B. C. Buch für grosse Kinder* (2 vols., Vienna, 1782).
10. *Ibid.*, I, 4.
11. *Ibid.*, p. 6.
12. *Ibid.*
13. *Ibid.*, p. 15.

Bauer. The only reason for his existence is that he should be in the position of giving up two-thirds of his income to his lord.[14]

Durst. The thirst for honor among soldiers is not to be stilled.[15]

Gesetz. The greater the number of laws, the more disorder ensues. Moreover, it is a calumny to suggest, as has been done, that new legislation in Vienna is introduced at eleven in the morning and ceases to be enforced at noon. The law forbidding the reckless driving of horse-drawn vehicles in the city was observed for almost three days.[16]

Junker. Happy that village in which the lord confines himself to hunting rabbits and boars, and not on occasion also his peasants.[17]

Igel. A leech will suck up only so much blood as it can hold. But a leech in a government office is just not to be filled up.[18]

Luft. Lovers are commonly believed to be able to live on air; why can't the poor do the same?[19]

Untersuchung. Etymologically considered, this means to look below, consequently not above. This is why most investigations turn up so little.[20]

In an epilogue to his little dictionary, Richter denied that it had any moralizing intent. He had only meant to have a little fun. Whatever his readers may have thought of this disclaimer, they were either amused or instructed enough to be moved to buy up a large edition of the work within a few days. In consequence, its author at once took advantage of what looked like a sure-fire market to bring out a second volume. For unknown reasons the tone of this was more moderate than that of the first, the targets were less prominent, the shafts not as barbed, there was

14. *Ibid.,* p. 16.
15. *Ibid.,* p. 21.
16. *Ibid.,* p. 39.
17. *Ibid.,* p. 51.
18. *Ibid.*
19. *Ibid.,* p. 64.
20. *Ibid.,* p. 97.

some obvious flattery of the monarch, and much more in the way of straightforward praise of specific reforms of Joseph's. There was even an explicitly anti-democratic note or two. To give just a few examples:

Bad. Since bakers have been ducked in cold water for cheating on the weight of bread, full-measure loaves are once more available.[21]

Einführen. The common people are so suspicious of all innovations that they will not even tolerate measures which are clearly designed to improve their lot.[22]

Hut. The Viennese have taken to wearing hats à la Washington. This, however, cannot be regarded as a serious threat to England, as out of a hundred wearers of such headgear, one at most would be able to tell you who Washington is.[23]

There are, to be sure, also some echoes of the first volume:

Invaliden. Soldiers are extremely useful: although their professional efforts bring about a diminution of the population in wartime, in times of peace, by redoubling their efforts, they succeed in making good the losses they have caused.[24]

Nächster. People of wealth and distinction apply this term to those who surround them. As these others are in the nature of things also rich, and as they take care not to let a poor man approach them too closely, they are unhappily deprived of the opportunity ever to help their needy neighbor.[25]

Pfänder. Private lenders are restricted to charging 4 percent interest per annum. The government lending bureau charges 10, but makes up for this by allowing the poor only one-third of the real value of the objects they pawn, presumably so that they will find it that much easier to redeem them.[26]

Zuchthaus. This is an institution devoted to the correction of

21. *Ibid.*, II, 13.
22. *Ibid.*, p. 24.
23. *Ibid.*, p. 37.
24. *Ibid.*, p. 41.
25. *Ibid.*, p. 68.
26. *Ibid.*, p. 72.

its inmates, whose purpose is somewhat vitiated by the well-known fact that practically all of them leave it with markedly worse characters than those they came in with.[27]

The rapacity of landlords, the brutality of soldiers, the indifference and inefficiency of officials—all come under attack. The intolerable condition of the poor is a recurrent theme. Not even Joseph's pet project of making it possible for them to survive hard times by pawning their property at a government agency, the *Versatzamt*, popularly called the Dorotheum, is spared. The overall effect is only to a degree mitigated by the obvious back-pedaling of the second volume. Taken as an entity, the *A. B. C. Buch* is a daring document, invested with particular significance because, rather than dealing in theories and abstractions, it addresses itself to concrete problems familiar to all its readers.

From this considerable success, Richter went on to edit a daily newspaper, *Die Brieftasche*, which attempted to bring the message of the *A. B. C. Buch* to a broader, less sophisticated, and poorer audience. Perhaps because it was not possible to keep up the level of wit and invention that had distinguished the book in face of the demands of supplying daily copy, perhaps because the poor were not ready to read about their troubles and the rich tired of hearing about them, the paper failed after only fifty issues.[28] Richter, it seems, lost a considerable amount of money in the venture and was correspondingly bitter about it. A year later his failure still rankled, and he denounced the Viennese reading public in a vicious satire. What right-thinking man, he asked, would not prefer to live as a beggar in Vienna than as a nobleman anywhere else? The Viennese were so virtuous that they deserved nothing less than that already-broiled chickens should fly straight into their open mouths. He closed by offering them a

27. *Ibid.*, p. 95.

28. Wurzbach, *Biographisches Lexicon*, XXVI, 58. Richter was also associated with two other short-lived newspapers, *Die Wiener Musterkarte* and *Der Wienerische Zuschauer*, but the degree of his involvement is uncertain. At any rate, the by no means negligible sum of 1,000 florins which he had earned on the *A.B.C. Buch* was soon dissipated. See Zitzenbacher, *Joseph Richter*, p. 17.

text for one of their beloved *Heurigen-Lieder,* dripping with idiocy, smugness, and self-satisfaction: "Wohl mir, dass ich ein Wiener bin, dass ich in Wien geboren."[29] It is probably best to pass over without comment the fact that this song became a favorite of pleasure-seeking Viennese wine-tipplers, and can still be heard today at any *Heurigen.*

At about the same time, Richter established his credentials as an anti-clerical. He published a little book attacking fasts, processions, ecclesiastical music, auricular confession, elaborate funerals, the cult of dubious saints, missions, festivals, indulgences, and monastic orders. The true Catholic, he said, who in his heart had long abhorred these abuses, could not help but rejoice that they were at last being remedied by Joseph's wise reforms.[30] But somehow Richter's heart wasn't in this sort of thing. The booklet hardly went beyond the repetition of trite and stale abstractions, and contained none of the accurate and poisonous observations that had become his stock-in-trade. It was probably simply a case of a lagging interest in religious questions. Unlike many of his friends and contemporaries, although he unquestionably supported Joseph's reform of the church, he never became a deist, and probably remained a reasonably orthodox, if reform-minded, Catholic all his life.

Richter's discouragement did not last indefinitely. By 1785 he was prepared to try his luck at journalism again. Toward the end of the previous year he had brought out another little book dealing with the foibles of the Viennese in the form of a child's catechism. He charged his fellow townsmen with an imposing gallery of crimes: they were immoral, naive, pretentious, lazy, always imitating the latest foreign craze (English picnics on the grass being the most recent), financially irresponsible, gluttonous, neglectful of their children, adulterous, and totally disinter-

---

29. J. Richter (F. Schmidt), *Vertheidigung der Wiener und Wienerinen* (Vienna, 1784).

30. J. Richter (Obermayer), *Bildergalerie katholischer Misbräuche* (Vienna, 1784), pp. 11ff.

ested in supporting the arts.[31] Whether it was because the portrait, although somewhat wart-ridden, was accurate, or because the Viennese preferred reading about their faults to worrying about the poor, this made Richter some money and also convinced him that there was a market for a satirical review addressing itself to the right audience.[32] The message would simply have to be interwoven with the sort of material that was likely to appeal to the sort of public that could afford to buy his paper.

The *Eipeldauer Briefe*, a satirical monthly that Richter brought out beginning in 1785, was an instant success.[33] It was to exist for over a quarter of a century, an unheard of longevity for a periodical publication in those days, and Richter himself was to remain on as editor-in-chief for better than half that period. After the death of Leopold II in 1792 the journal became a semi-official publication, receiving a subsidy from the government, and was depended upon to popularize the official position on important issues. But right from the start Richter in fact got a government subsidy for the *Eipeldauer Briefe*. This was represented as a *Gnadegehalt*, an honorarium of sorts, but in reality came out of a secret slush fund administered by the minister of police, Count Pergen.[34] Whatever the purpose of this arrangement was, it did not entirely prevent Richter from giving free rein to his comic bent.

The device that Richter used in the *Eipeldauer Briefe* was a traditional one, essentially a borrowing from Robinson Crusoe's

---

31. J. Richter, *Der gewöhnliche Wiener mit Leib und Seele* (Vienna, 1784).

32. The suggestion in Wurzbach (*Biographisches Lexicon*, XXIV, 57) that Richter's new journal was aimed chiefly at a lower-class reading public is absurd. It seems to be based exclusively on the fact that it was written in the Viennese dialect rather than in High German, but both bourgeoisie and aristocracy made a point of speaking *Wienerisch*. Indeed, even Maria Theresa had done so. Joseph and Sonnenfels were quite alone in their cult of High German.

33. J. Richter, *Die Eipeldauer Briefe: 1785–1797*, ed. E. v. Paunel (2 vols., Munich, 1917–18).

34. Nagl, Zeidler, and Castle, *Literaturgeschichte*, II, 293; Wurzbach, *Biographisches Lexicon*, XXVI, 58; Zitzenbacher, *Joseph Richter*, p. 15. The subsidy amounted to thirty florins a month.

man Friday. A rustic, naive and inexperienced in the ways of the world but uncommonly sharp-eyed, comes to Vienna. He writes to his cousin at home about what he observes. Here and there the editor steps in to correct what are obvious misapprehensions of his. The Eipeldauer's introduction to the great and modern metropolis is marred by little disappointments. The streets are full of holes, worse than in the countryside. He is told that street maintenance is the business of private entrepreneurs—what would happen to their profits if they were to fix every hole?[35] At the gates of the city he is searched by rude customs officials who do not bother to ask him if he has anything to declare until they have undressed him completely. By this time it is evening, and he makes his entry into the capital in the dark—the street lamps give off no more light than memorial candles in a church.[36] (This is a sly dig at Sonnenfels, who was inordinately proud of Vienna's street lighting, which had been installed under his direction.)

The next day the Eipeldauer goes to the police station to fill out his *Meldungszettel*. He reflects that this is an inherently silly procedure, because thieves or other malefactors are obviously not going to register under their real names. The editor here interjects the observation that not even government employees who sneak away from their posts in the provinces to spend a few days in Vienna do that.[37] Our rustic is amazed to hear that in the capital young ladies as well as gentlemen receive formal educations. To make up for this, he is told, they learn to cook and sew only after they have snared their men.[38] He goes on a walking tour of the

---

35. Richter, *Eipeldauer*, I, 1.
36. *Ibid.*, p. 2.
37. *Ibid.*
38. *Ibid.*, p. 6. The dominant female is a recurrent type in Richter's work. Magris (*Habsburgischer Mythos*, p. 36) suggests that his women dissolve in flirtatiousness, tenderness, and the melancholy of love, but lack strength and dynamism of the sort needed to transform the world. He adds that this is a dominant note throughout all of Austrian literature. Whatever one might think of the general proposition, it does not fit Richter. His women are eminently able to take care of themselves and their men.

city. Coming upon the imperial stables he is amazed to find that the horses are better lodged than the Emperor himself, not mentioning of course his less well-off subjects.[39] In the streets there are hordes of prisoners, hacking away at the ice which has accumulated. In a pretty little square three soldiers are tied to posts and are being given fifty lashes each, much to the delight and amusement of the large crowd that has gathered. In the next street, the Eipeldauer is knocked down by a speeding coach. A policeman who witnessed the scene is so saddened by the stupidity of people so evidently heedless of the safety of their fellow human beings that he immediately disappears from view. The editor explains that while this attribution of motive on the part of the Eipeldauer may be defensible, more probably it simply wasn't the man's post.[40]

After settling down in Vienna, the Eipeldauer meets the fate that sooner or later awaits all that city's residents: he becomes involved in a lawsuit. Not everything goes badly for him. He is fortunate in being let in to confer with his own lawyer after an insignificant wait of only an hour or two, as he has had the foresight to bring along a calf as a present. At this point the editor explains that the good attorney's conduct should not be taken amiss. Under Joseph's government lawyers have found their habitual means of supplementing their incomes illegally so reduced that they are hard put to make ends meet.[41]

As is readily apparent, the Eipeldauer's thrusts do not cut to the bone. He complains mostly about relative trivia, and his tone is one of gentle mockery rather than indignation. The social and political content of the letters is kept at a minimum. In the main, the customs and habits of the Viennese are held up to ridicule, not the institutions that govern them. The best thing that can be said about the Eipeldauer letters is that they were

39. Richter, *Eipeldauer*, I, 8.
40. *Ibid.*, pp. 14–18.
41. *Ibid.*, II, 21.

enormously popular. The Viennese, at least, were willing to laugh at themselves.

In 1787 Richter returned to more serious pursuits. In one major work and a series of minor ones he addressed himself to the question of Joseph's effectiveness as a ruler. If his objectivity can be questioned because of the government subsidy he was receiving, this is to an extent counterbalanced by the fact that, almost alone among his literary associates, he was neither a Mason nor a bureaucrat, and was thus presumably free of whatever prejudices were attendant upon either or both of these states.

By far the most important of Richter's political pronouncements are contained in a pamphlet which examines the question of why Joseph is unloved by his people.[42] The argument, being developed, as it was, by a man who was deeply committed to the success of the reform program but who was also sufficiently observant to perceive its tactical failures, deserves to be followed at some length. Richter admits that although there are men to be found in all classes of society who are deeply devoted to Joseph, the majority clearly does not love him. This can be perceived readily enough: his legislation evokes either opposition or, at best, general indifference; his public appearances generate no enthusiasm whatever among the people; the denunciations of Joseph that are printed every day and circulate everywhere have become so utterly vile as to beggar description. None of his indeed laudable reforms have succeeded in making him popular. (At this point Richter inserts a catalog of the Emperor's principal reforms to remind the Austrians of what he has already done for them.) Not even the fact that Joseph neither keeps expensive mistresses nor squanders his subjects' money on the building of elaborate palaces has resulted in his being loved.

What accounts for this paradox? If there is a mystery here, its resolution is close at hand:

42. J. Richter, *Warum wird Kaiser Joseph von seinem Volke nicht geliebt?*, in Gräffer, *Josephinische Curiosa*, I, 48–65.

1. Joseph's ecclesiastical reforms have intruded the authority of the state into a sphere that hitherto had been the private preserve of the clergy. Small wonder that most churchmen hate him and lose no opportunity to stir up their parishioners against him.

2. Joseph's laws limiting aristocratic privilege alienate not only a large proportion of that class but a host of lesser folk whose existences depend on the good will of the nobles.

3. The Emperor's own officials despise him because he requires an honest day's work of them in exchange for their pay.

4. The merchants of Vienna are unhappy because the prohibitions on foreign imports have cut heavily into their profits.

5. Domestic manufacturers who, it might be reasonable to expect, would profit from this arrangement are nevertheless resentful of the Emperor's refusal to grant them monopolies that would fill their pockets even more.

6. Lawyers and judges suffer, because while formerly they could count on being able to pad their incomes at the expense of litigants, now they are subject to close controls.

What could still be done by Joseph to redeem the situation, to regain the love of his people and thereby strengthen his program?

1. Joseph would do well to liberalize his unnecessarily tight-fisted pension policy, particularly where widows of state servants are involved.

2. He should treat his ministers less as servants and more as trusted friends: he is all too apt to forget that they are not soldiers who expect to be ordered about at will.

3. He should reverse his decision that even the most worthy and charitable institutions run by monastic orders, such as the Hospital of St. John, must be dissolved.

4. He should break himself of the habit, invariably unfortunate in its consequences, of rewarding his generals by giving them important posts in the civil administration.

5. He should abandon the practice of drafting the sons of the urban bourgeoisie into the army. Burghers who spend their good

money to educate their sons do not do this so that they may end up as soldiers.

6. The law requiring that suicides be buried in mass paupers' graves should be repealed. It punishes not the perpetrators of the act but their surviving families.

7. Joseph should make an effort to introduce into legal practice, if not actually into law, more in the way of differentiation in the treatment of occasional offenders as opposed to that meted out to hardened criminals.

8. In general, he should show a little more indulgence for human failings, and not insist, for instance, that the dead must be buried in sacks, a highly functional but vastly unpopular measure.

9. People of quality should not be punished in full view of the populace by being made to sweep the streets of the capital. The result of such a practice, inevitably, is a complete loss of respect on the part of the common people not only for those being punished but also for the principle of a structured society.

10. Joseph should pay his bureaucrats a living wage.

11. He should not persist in firing them without even pension rights merely because they turned out to be incompetent.

12. He should not carry his economies to the point of parsimony.

13. He should look into the question of whether some of his laws, instead of alleviating the economic ills of the country, did not instead increase the number of the poor.

14. He should refrain from behaving precipitously. On more than one occasion the over-hasty introduction of a law has brought about chaotic conditions.

15. He should break himself of the most unfortunate habit of being forever influenced in his judgments of men by denunciations.

16. He should make an attempt to reduce the ever-increasing amount of paper work, without which no official act could even be contemplated any longer.

17. He should show more respect and appreciation for the arts and sciences. It is a national disgrace to encounter unemployed artists, and to hear that writers who have earned the gratitude of the nation by propagating the enlightenment are starving.

It is of course apparent that there is practically no connection between Richter's diagnosis and the cures he suggests. He attributes Joseph's unpopularity exclusively to his repeated violations of the selfish and vested interests of the privileged classes rather than to any shortcomings inherent in his program. Yet the advice he gives him is evidently meant to demonstrate the often arbitrary and indeed thoughtless nature of many of the reforms, and even more particularly the damaging effect that Joseph's impetuosity and pettiness of character often have imparted to the whole of the program. The pamphlet assuredly is no attack on enlightened despotism. It merely expresses a heartfelt wish for a more agreeable despot.

In the same year that saw the appearance of this tally-sheet of Josephinism, Richter also published a novel, yet another *Entwicklungsroman*.[43] The hero, young Kaspar, having been thrown out of the Franciscans for various transgressions against the rule of the order, tries soldiering as a career. He is soon appalled at the stupidity and brutality that crop up at every turning in the military, and takes the first opportunity that offers itself to leave the army. He has heard that in the civil service many brilliant careers have been made by people innocent of the least ability, and manages to get taken on in a government office. His expectations have not been false. His colleagues, instead of working, stand around idly, taking snuff, exchanging gossip. It does not take much for them to sit down to a game of cards in the middle of the working day, or even to leave the office in order to go bowling. He never sees his superiors, who prefer to perform their duties in absentia. Out of pure boredom Kaspar decides to apply

43. J. Richter, *Herr Kaspar* (Vienna, 1787).

himself to his work and soon finds himself spoken of in awe throughout the service: a bureaucrat who actually works. Altogether, the book confines itself to this sort of mildly entertaining and hardly trenchant critique of official life, in fact a fictionalization of Joseph's famous *Hirtenbrief*, in which he had exhorted his officials to make greater efforts.

Also in 1787 Richter published a book of prayers appropriate to Joseph's situation, no more than an apologia for the Emperor, and a slight one at that. This was followed by another pamphlet which described Maria Theresa's return from the world of the dead. She approved of most of what she saw, but urged her son to profit from her wise examples in humanity and forbearance.[44] In 1789 he wrote a life of Frederick II of Prussia, which was taken seriously by some critics but was quite obviously a spoof meant to counteract the cult of the late king that was already developing in some quarters.[45] Thereafter he confined himself more and more to bringing out the *Eipeldauer Briefe*, which over the years became increasingly innocuous.

Richter's intellectual development runs in a direction contrary to that taken by almost all of his colleagues, who began as adherents of Joseph, became disillusioned with what they considered the incomplete nature of his reforms, hoped to go beyond him, and were after his death called to order by a frankly reactionary government. Richter's critics who assail him for having given lip service to the Franciscan reaction miss the point. He had changed his mind about Josephinism no later than 1785. There is no trace of the social and political radicalism of the *A. B. C. Buch* in the *Eipeldauer*. And the strictures on Joseph in the pamphlet of 1786 are inspired almost more by a conservative than by a liberal sentiment. This, incidentally, makes it seem unlikely, as might otherwise be assumed under the circumstances, that he had quite simply been bribed to change his opinions.

44. J. Richter, *Kaiserin Maria Theresia's Wiederkehr nach der Oberwelt* (Vienna, 1788). Cf. Wurzbach, *Biographisches Lexicon*, XXVI, 58.

45. Paunel, intro., *Eipeldauer Briefe*, I, xli.

Apart from the obvious fact that the sum of thirty florins a month would hardly have been sufficient to accomplish this end, the attacks on Joseph are too accurate to have issued from a bought pen. Richter appears to have become genuinely disillusioned. In his eyes Joseph's rather brutal and primitive methods had thrown away the opportunity of having a real impact on the Austrian situation. Moreover, perhaps a society which was above all else frivolous, always cheerful, but quite irresponsible was just not to be reformed. Increasingly, Richter's response to the problems of society became a mixture of pessimism and satirical amusement.[46] Austria would merely go on as long as it would go on. Every wise man knew that this would not be forever, but it was too much to expect the Viennese to worry about that. As for the social ideals of the *A. B. C. Buch,* they were evidently meant for a more serious-minded people.

46. This time Magris (*Habsburgischer Mythos,* p. 37) is dead right.

8 Jacobins and Enlightenment

IT IS easier to write about revolutions that took place than
about those that did not. Great events have a way of describing
themselves. They also validate, ex post facto, a detailed examination of even minute rivulets—enough of these might eventually
produce a new perspective. The same procedures in cases where
nothing in fact happened may very well fail to negotiate the narrow passage between mere antiquarianism and a purely tendentious, or at least highly selective, kind of history. Yet the *révolution manquée* of the early 1790's, if it did not in the last event
enlist very many Austrians in its ranks, captured the imagina-
tions of those against whom it would have been made; and this
sufficiently so that it served, over a long span of time, as the governing myth in justification of the repressive regime of Francis
II, a government whose reactionary mood is popularly but mistakenly thought to have been only a reaction to events in France.
So far as this is the case, it may be justifiable to spill a lot of ink
in the description of events which in themselves amounted to
very little.

Before events overtook theories in the course of the French
Revolution of 1789–94, in the German-speaking countries the
speculative horizon of even advanced political thinkers was severely limited. They were aware, of course, that chaos had in the
past occasionally followed general peasant uprisings, and might
do so again, but in general they refused to consider such relapses

into barbarism as having anything to do with viable political alternatives, to be included in rational calculations. The dominant political strain was what has been referred to in this context as liberalism, a school of thought which regarded the state as the last instance, not only to be preserved at all costs as the only effective hedge against anarchy, but because it was the only instrument capable of bringing about whatever reforms the body politic required. To be sure, the state of which they spoke was a somewhat idealized version of the real thing, a prefiguration of the later, also only ideal, *Rechtstaat,* but it was nevertheless a proper eighteenth-century state with a monarch at its head.[1] The radicals, those who, although willing in principle to retain monarchy, wished to reduce the ruler to a position of complaisant impotence, confining him to presiding as decoratively as possible over a state run in accordance with their theories, were few in number and had almost no influence. In Austria their position was additionally compromised by the Josephinian reforms, which for a time at least very effectively stole their thunder. Republicans were practically nonexistent.

But even in the 1780's there were in Austria men who were beginning to transcend the ideological limits of enlightened despotism in their speculations, either because they were encouraged by concessions made by a government which, although in appearance only, was not as absolute as it had formerly been, or because they were temperamentally unable to reconcile themselves to the permanent necessity of being limited in their political dreams by the not always reasonable whims of a prince. The Austrian Jacobinism of the 1790's, whatever it may have amounted to, was not merely derivative, not just another instance of the latest French fashion being aped mindlessly. It had native roots.

It is seldom useful, when discussing political movements, to think in terms of conspiracies and plots. Even where there hap-

---

1. F. Valjavec, *Die Entstehung der politischen Strömungen in Deutschland: 1770–1815* (Munich, 1951), pp. 37–39, 54.

pen to be conspirators and plotters, their influence is infrequent-
ly as pervasive as they themselves believe. Yet the fact remains
that the Austrian radicals seem, almost without exception, to
have known one another rather well over many years, and to
have adopted something of a conspiratorial manner in their behavior. For reasons which are not altogether clear, the great majority of them seem to have been ex-Swabians. Perhaps Swabia
was in fact a hotbed of political radicalism, or perhaps it was
merely a case of a small nucleus of malcontents attracting like-
minded compatriots. A book which they seem to have much admired and which served them as a sort of ideological rallying
point was Wilhelm Ludwig Wekhrlin's *Reise durch Ober-
Deutschland,* a work that not only struck out in strong language
at the social iniquities characteristic of Theresan Austria, but
offered a political solution for them in the form of a utopia, describing a country in which the balance had been redressed and
the ruler was powerless to interfere with the workings of a now
ideally functioning society.[2]

The most prominent of the Vienna Swabians is without
doubt the printer and bookseller Georg Philipp Wucherer. His
origins are obscure and his date of birth is unknown, but he
seems to have come to Vienna sometime in the 1770's. His re-
quests to open a printing establishment were turned down repeatedly by the suspicious authorities, but this did not deter him
from going ahead anyway. Eventually he made a fortune in the
Nachdruck market, and afterward used some of this money to
publish what were doubtless the most uninhibited attacks on
Joseph that the whole of the *Broschürenflut* was to produce. As
these came off the presses, he had them taken to Hungary, from
where they were mailed back to him so that he could make a
claim that he was only selling foreign publications on commission. This device was so transparent that it could not for long

2. *Ibid.,* pp. 105–106.

have fooled the authorities, and it has been suggested that for un-known reasons Wucherer enjoyed the secret protection of Gott-fried van Swieten.[3]

However this may have been, Wucherer did not hesitate to put on sale the most virulent materials. In 1786 one of these pamphlets, probably written by Wucherer himself, called the Emperor "a moody and unpredictable tyrant who was in the habit of trampling human rights underfoot and who laughed at justice."[4] In the same year he published another pamphlet liken-ing Joseph to the *Hanswurst*, the stage clown long a favorite of the Viennese public, who, unlike most similar popular heroes, achieved his triumphs not through guile or artfulness but through meanness of character and plain deceit.

What may have been Wucherer's most celebrated attack on Joseph followed upon the trial and execution of a Baron von Zahlheim. This gentleman of noble birth but restricted means had murdered his landlady in lieu of paying his rent, a murder accompanied by such grizzly circumstances that Joseph com-manded that the death penalty, which had in practice been sus-pended during his reign, be invoked. Accordingly, Zahlheim was broken on the wheel. Wucherer now produced a pamphlet, again almost certainly of his own authorship, which not only protested against the medieval barbarity of the punishment but argued, in the face of all the evidence, that Zahlheim had been the victim of a judicial murder: he had been convicted only because of the criminal ignorance of his judges, in itself merely a further symp-tom of a general breakdown of the judicial system. The citizen

3. Sashegyi, *Zensur und Geistesfreiheit*, p. 123; Wurzbach, *Biographisches Lexicon*, LVIII, 211; Gräffer, *Josephinische Curiosa*, III, 64; E. Wangermann, *From Joseph II to the Jacobin Trials* (2nd ed., Oxford, 1969), p. 41; Silagi, *Jakobiner*, p. 48.

4. *Freymüthige Bemerkungen über des Verbrechen und die Strafe des Garde-Obristleutnant Szekely*, quoted in Rautenstrauch's attack on Wucherer in Gräffer, *Josephinische Curiosa*, III, 81–82. It is in a way remarkable how little the vo-cabulary of the radical left for expressing formal outrage has changed over two centuries.

no longer enjoyed the protection of the law; he was at the mercy of an arbitrary and relentless regime.[5]

Wucherer also was in contact with the Prussian radical Karl Friedrich Bahrdt, a leading critic of the repressive policies of Frederick William II. In order to further his aims Bahrdt founded a secret society with aggressively anti-aristocratic connotations. Wucherer presently became the head of the Austrian branch of this organization.[6] Further, Wucherer corresponded with the Swabian unfrocked priest Joseph Rendler about the possibility of bringing his works out in an Austrian edition. Rendler had written a *Disquisition on the Rights and Obligations of Men* which Wucherer described somewhat disingenuously as no more than the logical extension of Joseph's reform program, but which in fact, in the name of unfettered rationalism, proposed to abolish all existing governments. There was apparently a limit to the risks that even Wucherer was willing to take, because the Austrian edition never saw the light of day.[7]

Wucherer's downfall came in 1789, largely because of another pamphlet which he had written. Entitled *An Examination of the Proofs of the Christian Religion*, this did not stop at violent attacks on the church, but proceeded to call into question the whole of the Christian dogma.[8] Thereupon a police spy bought a copy of the offending work at Wucherer's shop and promptly arrested him. While he was being held in custody his

5. Gräffer, *Josephinische Curiosa*, III, 86; G. P. Wucherer, *Beweis, das Zahlheim als ein Opfer der Unwissenheit seiner Richter und durch Gewalt des Stärkeren hingerichtet wurde* (Ostahiti [Vienna], 1786). Cf. Gnau, *Die Zensur*, pp. 206–211.

6. Valjavec, *Strömungen*, p. 25; Wangermann, *Joseph II to the Jacobin Trials*, pp. 40–42; S. G. Flygt, *The Notorious Dr. Bahrdt* (Nashville, Tenn., 1963), *passim.*

7. H. Scheel, *Süddeutsche Jakobiner* (Berlin, 1962), p. 91.

8. Sashegyi, *Zensur und Geistesfreiheit*, p. 123. Wangermann (*Joseph II to the Jacobin Trials*, p. 41) maintains that Wucherer's difficulties with the authorities were the result of a decision on the part of Joseph and Pergen to suppress Bahrdt's society, which they regarded as a genuine threat to the government, but he offers no convincing evidence in support of such an interpretation.

premises were searched and a large number of books prohibited by the censorship was found. At this point, on Joseph's direct order, a fine of 1,000 florins was levied against Wucherer, the whole of his stock was pulped, and he was expelled from Austria as an undesirable alien.[9] The proceedings were probably illegal and Wucherer had undoubtedly been deprived of some of his rights under the law. It was a sign of a more general change in mood. As Joseph's health deteriorated, his seemingly endless patience with his critics was growing visibly shorter. Soon afterward the law on censorship, which for some time had been allowing anything at all to appear, the censors stepping in only subsequently in case of need, was again changed. Hereafter all manuscripts would once more have to be submitted to the censor before publication.[10]

Apart from this, one looks almost in vain for anything resembling organized radical activity in Austria before 1789. Whether the Klagenfurt salon of Baron Franz de Paula von Herbert, in which opponents of "shallow Josephinism" met to steep themselves in Kantian philosophy, had radical implications remains moot.[11] There were, to be sure, cases of individual radicalism. Insofar as this seems to have had a locus, it was, surprisingly, the University of Vienna, long dormant but now, in the late evening of Joseph's reign, at last beginning to look outside its walls. In November, 1789, among a number of theses defended in a public disputation organized by the faculty of theology, there was one which argued that "the monarch who deliberately and by force acts in a sense contrary to the common good is a tyrant against whom the people, in defense of their basic rights, may protect themselves."[12]

In the same year a doctoral thesis accepted in the faculty of

9. Wangermann, *Joseph II to the Jacobin Trials*, pp. 41–42.
10. Sashegyi, *Zensur und Geistesfreiheit*, p. 125.
11. Nussbaumer, *Geistiges Kärnten*, p. 274.
12. Wiedemann, "Bücher-Censur," p. 343.

philosophy on the subject of Roman laws governing interest rates went rather beyond the immediate topic and maintained, among other propositions, that all government rests ultimately and only on the authority granted it by a social contract; that the monarch is obliged to obey the law just like any other citizen of the state; that fundamental laws can be changed only with the consent of the governed; and that the ruler who ignores these basic propositions may be lawfully opposed. Joseph, to whose attention this document was brought, made some reference to "the contemporary trumpery concerning liberty and independence which might in some circumstances be dangerous to the state" and ordered that thereafter dissertations should confine themselves to their subjects.[13] There were also complaints about two professors of history at the university, Watteroth and Dannemeyer, who, in the course of insisting on the universal primacy of reason, were subjecting existing institutions to too close a scrutiny.[14]

While none of this can, in truth, be regarded as even the formative stage of a radical party, it is at least an indication that there was a certain predisposition to accept radical ideas when they began to be exported from France in quantity. Evidence of such influences first came to light in the course of 1790. The Viennese police uncovered a club, drawing its membership from household servants of French nationality, several even in the employ of Prince Kaunitz, which met irregularly to discuss the events taking place in France, and possible ways and means of encouraging appropriate elements of the Austrian population to imitate the example of the French.[15] Also, a poem by Christian Schubart, mocking the Germans for their lack of will and their obvious reluctance to follow in the wake of France, was making the rounds of Vienna: "Denn kalte, frostige Natur schickt sich

---

13. Kink, *Kaiserlichen Universität*, I/1, 587.
14. *Ibid.*, I/2, 297–300.
15. Gräffer, *Josephinische Curiosa*, III, 178.

allein für arme deutsche Sclaven."[16] In Silesia I. A. Fessler, moving back and forth between the Prussian and Austrian parts of the province, attempted to rally his old Illuminati friends on behalf of the French Revolution, but without much success.[17]

The Hapsburg monarchy was very close to revolution in 1790, but not to a revolution on the French model. Rather, a Hungarian national uprising, directed against Joseph's attempts to centralize the government of that country, threatened. The Hungarians, who were receiving financial support from Prussia and probably had been promised more direct help should they require it, on January 28, 1790, forced the dying Joseph to repeal practically all of his reforms for Hungary.[18] There was nothing in any of this to enlist the sympathies of either the Austrian liberals or the radicals. Nobiliar opposition to an overly ambitious central power might, in some circumstances, produce attitudes congenial to the development of political liberalism, but the Hungarian magnates simply did not inspire much confidence in any but the most retrograde of political thinkers.

A genuine Austrian Jacobin conspiracy did not emerge until 1794. Insofar as it can be reconstructed from the scarce evidence available, it seems to have been foremost a reaction against the war with revolutionary France which was going about as badly as possible, although, as there were several groups of conspirators, their motives may not in all cases have been identical.[19] Paradoxically also, the Austrian Jacobins may have been encouraged, at least indirectly, by the government itself in the brief reign of Leopold II, who attempted to foster the growth of democratic institutions in Hungary in order to pit them against the

16. *Ibid.*, p. 179.

17. J. Droz, *L'Allemagne et la Révolution Française* (Paris, 1949), p. 96.

18. C. A. Macartney, *The Habsburg Empire: 1790–1918* (London, 1968), p. 133.

19. For detailed treatments of the Austrian Jacobin conspiracy, see Silagi, *Jakobiner*, pp. 177–183; Wangermann, *Joseph II to the Jacobin Trials*, pp. 137–156; and W. C. Langsam, "Emperor Francis II and the Austrian 'Jacobins,' 1792–1796," *American Historical Review*, L (1945).

inordinate political pretensions of the Hungarian magnates.[20] Ultimately, evidences of Jacobin activity were uncovered in Graz, Innsbruck, and Vienna. The Innsbruck affair seems to have been the most ephemeral. A group of young students, inspired by the Italian valet of a visiting English lord, dedicated themselves to the cause of liberty and equality, but undertook no steps to secure the implementation of this goal.[21] In Graz, Jacobinism apparently became intertwined with the purely local issue of increased representation for the lower orders in the Styrian Estates, and it is exceedingly difficult to decide which of the issues was paramount in the mind of those who agitated for an increase in liberty. Here too there were no results to speak of.[22]

In Vienna there appear to have been at least three different groups of Jacobins. The intermediary between them and those of a like mind in Hungary was a Count Stanislaus Soltyk, a representative of the Polish patriot and revolutionary leader Thaddeus Kościuszko. The least obscure of the Viennese Jacobins were Baron Andreas Riedel, a former government servant under Leopold II, and a Lieutenant Franz Hebenstreit, who had served at various times in both the Austrian and Prussian armies. Mostly, these groups limited their activities to interminable discussions of what the implications of the latest developments in the always rapidly changing French situation might be. Occasionally they sang the Eipeldauer song, although never in public. This was a piece of doggerel, composed either by Hebenstreit himself or by a man named Beck, which accused the Emperor Francis of having made common cause with the aristocrats, a proceeding that had proved fatal to Louis XVI; all good Austrians were urged to see to it that a similar fate overtook their ruler.[23]

What most distinguished the members of these more or less interlocking conspiracies was their total lack of prominence.

---

20. See D. Silagi, "Ungarn und der geheime Mitarbeiterkreis Kaiser Leopolds II.," *Südosteuropäische Arbeiten*, LVII (1961).
21. Wangermann, *Joseph II to the Jacobin Trials*, p. 138.
22. *Ibid.*
23. *Ibid.*, pp. 139–140; Silagi, *Jakobiner*, pp. 179–180.

Not one of the important literati or social critics of the Josephine period had the least connection with them.[24] Yet neither were they persons of no consequence whatever. Among them were the seventeen-year-old Count Sigismund von Hohenwart, the aulic councilor Franz Gotthardi, the dean of the School of Veterinary Medicine of the University of Vienna, Dr. Johann Gottlieb Wollstein, and the sometime poet Martin Joseph Pranstätter.[25] The most prominent of the Hungarian Jacobins, the ex-abbot Ignatz Joseph Martinovics, frequently came to Vienna to confer with these men. He had been employed for a time under Leopold II in conducting sensitive probings to determine to what extent the authority of the Hungarian Estates might be bypassed, and was for that reason still regarded as a person of influence in Austria. Because of the always latent separatist sentiments in Hungary, never requiring anything but a minimal excuse to be activated, Martinovics' conspiracy, when it was finally uncovered by the authorities, was regarded as potentially very dangerous. It may have been all of that. In Austria, however, the Jacobins were able, so far as is known, to produce no more than two overt acts in support of their principles.

On reflection, neither of these can be considered to have had a drastic influence on the course of subsequent events. On July 13, 1794, the Austrian Jacobins, for once united into a single body, traveled from Vienna to nearby Mödling and, in a sequestered valley not far removed from that little town, planted a tree of liberty. Emboldened by the consumption of not inconsiderable quantities of wine, the conspirators then sang some revolutionary songs, including the stirring *Die Zeiten, Brüder, sind nicht mehr, da Kron und Zepter gelten*. Afterward, Riedel read a manifesto calling for the immediate formation of an anti-aristocratic league which would at long last establish the com-

24. Wangermann's assertion (*Joseph II to the Jacobin Trials*, p. 139) that Blumauer belonged to a Jacobin circle is made without any supporting evidence whatever. His landlord, Johann Hackl, was alleged by the police to have belonged to the conspiracy, but this was apparently a mistake.

25. Langsam, "Francis II and the Jacobins," p. 477.

plete equality of all men. This having been accomplished, the participants repaired to their respective homes.[26]

The second incident of overt Jacobin activity unfolded as follows: in the spring of 1794 it had come to Count Soltyk's attention that Hebenstreit was claiming to have invented a revolutionary new war engine, something in the nature of a heavy gun protected by extraordinarily thick armor. Soltyk was anxious to secure this device for use by Kościuszko's party in Poland and approached the Viennese Jacobin leadership with a request for a copy of the plans. Their answer was that they would let him have them only if he could arrange for the transmission of another copy to the revolutionary government in Paris. A go-between in the person of the Lutheran preacher Karl Traugott Held was found, who, in the company of a medical student named Denkmann, took the plans to Freiburg. There they met a French general who sent them on to Paris with a letter of introduction to the minister of war, Carnot. They arrived in the French capital in May, 1794, in the midst of a highly charged political atmosphere, and were promptly arrested as Austrian spies. By the time Carnot had an opportunity to look into the matter and secure their release, the revolutionary government was within days of being overthrown. The Austrian secret weapon, which had not arrived in time to save it, disappeared into the files of the ministry. Nothing seems to have come of Hebenstreit's machine either in Poland or, after his arrest and the confiscation of his papers, in Austria.[27] Apparently expert military opinion judged that it would not work very well.

This, if one excepts a mysterious sheet of paper that was nailed to the principal door of the University of Vienna in July, calling on all students to join in the forthcoming revolution,[28] was the sum of Jacobin activity in Austria. It would have been

26. Macartney, *The Habsburg Empire*, p. 157; E. Winter, *Früliberalismus in der Donaumonarchie* (Berlin, 1968), p. 10; K. Gutkas, *Geschichte des Landes Nieder-Oesterreich* (3 vols., Vienna, 1959), III, 43.

27. Silagi, *Jakobiner*, pp. 177–178.

28. *Ibid.*, p. 179.

no more than a comic-opera interlude had not the minister of police, Count Johann Anton Pergen, and his assistant, Count Franz Joseph Saurau, either because they were convinced that the Jacobins constituted a real threat to the state's security or more likely in order to fan up the public's lagging enthusiasm for the war, decided that arrests would have to be made. They had been kept abreast of the conspiracy all along and in copious detail by the bookseller Joseph Vincenz Degen, a double agent. Degen was now instructed to try his luck as *agent provocateur* and in consequence arranged a meeting in the Augarten with Hebenstreit, who, after a little prodding and primed with a large mug of beer, unfolded a wild scheme for a revolution which was to begin with the seizure of the capital by three or four thousand radical students, who would overwhelm the sentries, break into the barracks, kill the officers, convince the soldiers to join them, murder all aristocrats, seize the Emperor himself, and after having forced him at sword's point to sign an appropriate number of cartes blanches, kill him too. Thereupon a provisional government would be proclaimed, whose first official act would be to abolish serfdom once and for all.[29] The plan, lacking only the three or four thousand revolutionary students to put it into effect, had all the lethal danger of Hebenstreit's war engine, although the provision for the rebels to get the Emperor's permission for their actions before doing away with him constitutes a nice touch. But there was no question about this being treasonable talk, and the Emperor Francis, who up to this point had been reluctant to proceed against the conspirators, gave the police permission to do so now. After a long and complicated trial, Hebenstreit was condemned to death and hanged and the others were given jail terms of varying lengths, from sixty years for Riedel to five months for Professor Wollstein, the veterinarian, upon whose training, it was argued, the state had spent so much money that it would have been economi-

29. Wangermann, *Joseph II to the Jacobin Trials*, pp. 155–156.

cally indefensible to keep him away from his post for any greater length of time.[30]

To maintain, even by implication, that any part of this absurd charade was the logical consequence of the Josephinian enlightenment is utter nonsense. It may even be doubted that the two phenomena were in any significant way related. While the Austrian intelligentsia did not simply disappear with the death of Joseph, it was not drawn into any Jacobin plots, nor was it even remotely sympathetic to them. The Jacobin conspiracy, rather than having been the finale, albeit aborted, of the Austrian enlightenment, was at best a meaningless distortion of it, a sideshow.

30. *Ibid.*, pp. 170–171.

9
Enlightenment and Josephinism

IN ORDER to understand what really happened to the Austrian *Aufklärer*, it becomes necessary to examine with more care than usual the relationship of their enlightened opinions to the enlightened despotism of Joseph. The problem has been largely a historiographical one. It has been put in a variety of ways, but usually not in such a manner that a reasonable answer could have emerged. The most primitive solution, and by far the one that has enjoyed the greatest longevity, has been to beg the question as pervasively as possible: Joseph, the sorcerer's apprentice of the French philosophes, imposed reforms on a disinterested and even reluctant country, trampled ancient privilege underfoot, and dragged Austria kicking and screaming into the eighteenth century. In other words, there was an attempted revolution from above which ultimately could not do anything but fail because of a complete lack of support from below, and because as opposition to his arbitrary methods developed, the Emperor came with the passing of every day to look more like a Stuart tyrant than like the benign and wise reformer which he wished to be.[1] Apart from being a complete misreading of

1. An early statement of this theory may be found in W. Wenck, *Deutschland vor hundert Jahren* (2 vols., Leipzig, 1887, 1890), I, 48. It constitutes the bulk of the argument of two of the better-known biographies of Joseph: S. K. Padover, *The Revolutionary Emperor: Joseph II of Austria* (2nd ed., New York, 1967), and F. Féjtö, *Un Hapsbourg révolutionnaire: Joseph II* (Paris, 1953). Its most recent airing has been in F. Schreyvogl, *Ein Jahrhundert zu früh: Das Schicksal Josephs II.* (Vienna, Berlin, and Stuttgart, 1964).

Joseph's character and intentions, this theory labors under the additional disadvantage of positing a country devoid of sufficient intellectual and political sophistication to appreciate the import of Joseph's plans. As has probably been demonstrated plainly enough, such an analysis does not correspond to the facts.

A rather more subtle version of this theory evolved toward the beginning of the present century. Joseph's ideas were shown to have been derived from a blend of the teachings of the natural-law school of Grotius, Pufendorf, and Christian Wolff, with the influence of the Italian Catholic reform party of Muratori and his circle. In addition, he was supposed to have been continually prodded toward greater effort by men such as Justi and Martini. Thus, in sum, his reign was actually the culmination of the efforts of a small party of doctrinaire liberals to impose their views of society on Austria.[2] This had the advantage of replacing the myth of Joseph the idiosyncratic despot with that of the dictatorship of the *Zeitgeist,* a concept then much in vogue, but otherwise did not come appreciably closer to the facts of the case. This interpretation soon came under attack for ignoring the obvious, namely that it was impossible to demonstrate from the available evidence, by no means slight, that Joseph subscribed to any systematic body of doctrine. If he could be considered to have been devoted to anything, it was nothing more mysterious than *Realpolitik.*[3]

While this view of Joseph as the essentially uncomplicated practical politician was initially rejected as amateurish and heretical, it gradually gained general acceptance when it came to be buttressed by more systematic studies of the Theresan period. It was now maintained that the loss of Silesia, or the military defeat at the hands of Prussia in two wars, or both, had occasioned something like a cultural shock in Austria. Not only the

2. Voltelini, "Naturrechtlichen Lehren und Reformen," *passim.*
3. G. Holzknecht, *Ursprung und Herkunft der Reformideen Kaiser Josefs II. auf kirchlichem Gebiete* (Innsbruck, 1914), pp. 2ff.

monarch but important segments of the governing classes were alleged to have been swept away by the notion that the unfavorable verdict of the Silesian Wars must at all costs be reversed, even if this meant tampering with ancient and hitherto sacrosanct institutions. And once one began to make changes, it became quickly evident that a veritable chain of necessary events had to follow in order that the beneficial effects of the original innovations might not be lost in a swamp of inertia.

Later and more elaborated versions of the same theory held that, in addition, there were also more ancient impulses toward modernization, going back at least to the reign of Leopold I (1658–1705); indeed, that the accretions to the royal power that any successful attempt at centralization brought with it were in themselves steps toward modernity. Still, the basic impulse behind the Josephinian reforms was held to have been entirely empirical.[4] While there may be much underlying truth in these views, they do have the undoubted disadvantage of doing away with, and not merely by implication, whatever influence the enlightenment may have had on its surroundings. Thus, the philosophes of all nations were engaged in a continuing exercise of self-delusion: it suited their vanity to believe that their mere pronouncements moved monarchs to action; they were too unworldly to realize that men who hold great power are merely concerned with the very pragmatic problem of how best to keep it.[5] "Many philosophers wrote with the aim of converting rulers. Many philosophers of the eighteenth century believed that they had succeeded. Some lived to be disillusioned."[6] While there is something seductive about the austere simplicity of such opinions—most intellectuals suspect in secret that their hold on reality is tenuous and their chances of influencing it are nil—they have a way of corresponding rather too neatly with the

4. For instance, G. Lefèbvre, "Le Despotisme éclairé," *Annales Historiques de la Révolution Française,* XXI (1949), 98, 109.

5. *Ibid.,* p. 110.

6. Wangermann, *Joseph II to the Jacobin Trials,* p. 1

political predilections of their authors. It has more than once been said that nothing can stop an idea whose time has come, and as the time for liberalism had obviously not arrived in eighteenth-century Austria, there is clearly not much point in wasting one's time on examining the ideas of those who had been foolish enough to delude themselves into believing that it had.

But it will not do simply to legislate the *Aufklärer* out of existence. They lived, they wrote, and they had readers, some of whom lived in palaces and may very well have been influenced by what they read. The question of what the nature and extent of such influences might have been remains. At least there has been no scarcity of suggested answers. Some of them have contributed materially to a better understanding of the problem, and it will prove useful to enumerate and discuss them.

1. The Austrian intelligentsia, although not without influence, was made up almost exclusively of a very narrow segment of the upper classes. Its real importance lay in the diffusion of the German classics in Austria, works of a higher merit than had previously been known there and thus capable of extending the narrow horizon of the Austrian intellectual world.[7]

2. The Josephinian party was made up of a combination of bureaucrats, members of the intelligentsia, persons belonging to both the upper and middle bourgeoisie, and considerable numbers of the clergy. All these men were not only well grounded in the literature of the enlightenment, but were also influenced by dimly adumbrated views of the future. What these may have been is not made explicit, but as they seem to have affected the "economically active" bourgeoisie most profoundly, it can be assumed that some sort of vision of a social order in which economic interests and distinctions are paramount is meant.[8]

3. Josephinism was above all the practical realization of Kant's categorical imperative. Thus, whatever moral advan-

---

7. Müller, "Absolutismus," pp. 22, 36.
8. Valjavec, *Der Josefinismus*, pp. 20–21.

tages it may have enjoyed, it faced the hopeless task of trying to impose an essentially foreign, Prussian-Protestant ideal on Austria. Moreover, as Joseph conceived of literature principally as a didactic tool in the service of the all-powerful state, the poet was to be a bureaucrat not only in fact, but was meant to think of himself principally as one. This circumstance led to the development of a class of pseudo-intellectuals, eclectics, and autodidacts, motivated by the discipline and obedience more usually to be found among noncommissioned officers to propagate that part of the enlightenment most useful to the state as best they could. In the final analysis, the whole movement was a negation of the Austrian spirit, which would find its true expression again only in romanticism.[9]

4. The Josephinian intelligentsia was in fact the articulate tip of the bourgeois iceberg. It never succeeded in playing a significant political role because of a basic contradiction in its essence: the times still belonged to absolute monarchy but, as the histories of both Prussia and Russia had demonstrated, the absolute monarch could accomplish his aims only by contracting an alliance with the feudal aristocracy. To try to govern against it with support from the bourgeoisie was to court disaster for both parties to such an alliance. By doing so, Joseph had paved the way to an inevitable feudal reaction.[10]

5. Josephinism was only very distantly related to the *Aufklärung*. Its main thrust was a centralizing one which, as it necessarily affected the church, had inevitable consequences for the Austrian intellectuals. Coinciding as it did with the dissolution of the Jesuits, it cut many clerics loose from their moorings. The berths which they found in various state offices were, for them, not generally acceptable substitutes. These men were spiritual drifters, the flotsam of a culture in the process of being broken up. They tried to bring to the service of the state the

9. J. A. Lux, *Ein Jahrtausend österreichischer Dichtung* (2nd ed., Vienna, 1948).

10. Lefèbvre, "Despotisme éclairé," p. 113.

same spiritual dedication with which they had served the church, but often only with indifferent success, as their commitment to the enlightenment did not go very deep.[11]

6. It is most unfortunate that the myth of Joseph the revolutionary from above has been succeeded by the no less mythical "Josephinian spirit." There were real, identifiable Josephinists, who, if they are not always easy to identify, nevertheless existed. Their unifying characteristic was a dedication to the ideal of the state that approached idolatry.[12]

7. Josephinism was nothing more than *Staatskirchentum*, an attempt to secularize a still largely clerically dominated society. The example of Prussia, where the Protestant churches were meekly subservient to the authority of the state, was extremely seductive in the wake of the Seven Years' War. Prince Kaunitz, influenced also by the ideas of the Muratori circle which he had encountered in Lombardy, recruited from among officials and literati a party of willing hands whose work was to be the complete eradication of all clerical influence in Austria. Far from being the result of an accumulation of anonymous and mysterious forces, Josephinism is demonstrably the work of Kaunitz and his hired helpers.[13]

8. The tradition of giving unsolicited advice to princes was a very ancient one in the realms of the House of Habsburg. It is thus in no way surprising that the literati of the eighteenth century, when provided with an opening by the loosening of the censorship, should have availed themselves of the opportunity to produce a floodtide of advice. But by no means all of the Josephinist writers can be called enlightened. In all prob-

---

11. K. Eder, *Der Liberalismus in Altösterreich* (Munich and Vienna, 1955), pp. 40–54.

12. Bauer, "Le Joséphisme," pp. 628, 639.

13. H. Rieser, *Der Geist des Josephinismus* (Vienna, 1963), pp. 83–85. This is essentially a summary of Maass's *Josephinismus*, and the views expressed therein are almost without exception those of Maass. The latter has only slightly modified his opinions about the sole responsibility of Kaunitz in his latest work, *Der Frühjosephinismus* (Vienna and Munich, 1969).

ability the majority of them were mere bureaucrats who worked in support of the new direction with as much or as little zeal as they had mustered for the old. Those who were true *Aufklärer* only rarely approached the originality and intellectual power of their north German counterparts. But they did enjoy one great advantage over them, and indeed over the French philosophes: they were, up to a point, able to transform the state in accordance with their theoretical views. This gave them a sense of fulfillment and satisfaction unique among eighteenth-century intelligentsias.[14]

9. Sonnenfels and Martini, the heirs of a French tradition rather weakened by its passage through north German hands, developed the theory that humanity, at least in its Austrian form, had not matured sufficiently to make meaningful independent political decisions. Hence improvements would have to be forced upon it by those sufficiently enlightened to appreciate the need for them. This view corresponded perfectly with Joseph's intentions, which were not by any means to overthrow the old order, but rather to save what could be saved of it for the different world whose approach he perceived. But finding himself opposed at every turn by the nobility and clergy, he tried to find a basis of support elsewhere. These efforts met with enthusiastic acceptance both among bourgeoisie and lower nobility, which classes formed themselves into a rationalistic clique for all of his reforms. At his death, disoriented and unable to decide whether their interests lay in siding with the approaching reaction or in supporting the desperate attempts of the radicals to save the program, they lost all influence.[15]

10. And finally, we have the eclectic view that there was much of traditional absolutism and *Staatskirchentum* in Josephinism, but it was also the result of an attempt to broaden the base of royal power by forging alliances with the bourgeoisie and the

14. Zöllner, "Aufklärung und Josefinismus," pp. 208, 215–216.
15. K. Benda, "Probleme des Josephinismus und des Jakobinerthums in der Habsburgischen Monarchie," *Südost-Forschungen,* XXV (1966), pp. 40–49.

peasants in order to reduce the power of the nobility, and furthermore it was deeply influenced by the enlightenment.[16]

It can readily be seen that insofar as these interpretations do not contain elements that are mutually exclusive, they may well be profitably combined. The temptation to follow Eduard Winter in his latest eclectic mood is considerable. To be sure, the anti-clerical conspiracy theory seems both overdrawn and regressive. There were, after all, limits to Kaunitz' power, and to make him rather than Joseph the revolutionary from above seems to offer no very obvious improvement. The most important consideration is that there appears to be no good reason to give the Austrian *Aufklärer* shorter shrift than they deserve, either out of a political *parti pris* or out of an overly developed literary snobbery. To dismiss them as the timid spokesmen of an aborted bourgeois liberation movement, cowardly revolutionaries who were all too easily dissuaded from their appointed mission by a show of force, is to beg some important questions. It has by no means been established that most of these men were committed to, or were even conscious of representing, any sort of explicitly bourgeois ideology. Indeed, the bulk of the evidence points to a contrary assumption. And a by no means negligible fraction of these men were not members of the bourgeoisie at all, but belonged to the minor aristocracy. To what extent Josephinism was in actuality a gentry-oriented movement, an attempt not to dispossess the aristocracy but to shift the balance of power within it, is a question that has, so far, simply not been investigated at all.

While it would be absurd to maintain that in absolute literary merit, or in poetic grandeur, the Austrian literati were the equals of Goethe and Schiller, this is quite beside the point. The question is not whether they wrote for the ages, but whether they addressed themselves with some relevance to actually existing problems, and whether what they wrote was considered impor-

16. Winter, *Frühliberalismus*, p. 13. This is only the most recent of Winter's many pronouncements on the subject, and probably not his final word.

tant enough to be mulled over by their contemporaries. It would indeed be naive to assume that Joseph treated their writings, or for that matter anyone else's, as a sort of score from which to conduct his reform program. As should be clear by now, in many areas he did not even like to see any approbation of his policies. Yet the assumption that for that reason these men had no influence at all is equally naive. In spite of a penchant for the arbitrary, Joseph was neither an insensitive tyrant nor a calculating machine unable to register anything beside the advantages of the state. His reforms were demonstrably not based on a doctrinaire, carefully prepared scheme, but were more the result of essentially impressionistic and sometimes quite ad hoc soundings. In spite of his dislike for unsolicited advice, there can be no question but that he was susceptible to influences from the climate of opinion. And here the circumstance that the *Aufklärer* established a favorable climate for his reforms is of the first importance. Their activities created a resonance for his thought that prevented him from succumbing much earlier to the numbing despair, the result of the belated conviction that he was really Sisyphus and not Hercules, which gripped him in the last year of his life.

The Austrian *Aufklärer* were men whose political ambitions were, in a sense, as modest as their literary talents. They searched for a middle road between tyranny and slavery.[17] For this reason the spectrum of political remedies open to them was necessarily limited. It ranged from timid appeals to the ruler's sense of responsibility, through demands for the total abolition of the censorship, leading to an absolute freedom of the press which would, they believed, keep even a would-be tyrant in bounds by the constant threat of public exposure, to somewhat nebulous schemes for circumscribing the ruler's powers, reducing him, perhaps, to the position of a benevolent chairman of a board consisting of the wise men of the nation, a sort of dim prefiguration of the

17. J. Hermand, *Von Deutscher Republik: 1775–1795* (2 vols., Frankfurt a. M., 1968), I, 22–23.

never-realized German professorial republic. There was, on the whole, a notable absence of strong talk about priestly entrails and the strangling of kings. This, to be sure, has been adjudged a fault in an age which seems totally addicted to total solutions.

Thus, in the last analysis it will be seen that the faults and merits of the Austrian *Aufklärer* were essentially Austrian faults and merits. If their goals were too modest, and their means too timid, they were also largely free of fanaticism. If they had a tendency to toady to Joseph as the one symbol of authority, to tailor their suggestions to his known preferences, they were also capable of criticizing, even of mocking him. If there was a certain carelessness, not to say philistinism, about the systems they built, which in truth were anything but airtight, at least they were not disfigured by a doctrinaire devotion to ideology. It may be objected that the sum of these qualities results only in the celebrated Austrian *Schlamperei*, which here was particularly out of place as it prevented the body of men who, by their education and general cultural attainments, were best suited to lead the country into a brighter political future from taking appropriately determined action. In answer to such argument, one may point out two considerations: it is not reasonable to expect the Austrians, or any other people for that matter, to become what by nature they have never been; and although the *furia francese* may at times lead to the gaining of important objectives, it more often merely leaves the field of battle strewn with corpses.

In one other important respect the Austrian *Aufklärer* do not conform to the Procrustean tendencies of our age. By all rights they should have suffered from all the known symptoms of alienation. After all, most of them found it necessary to work at routine jobs to support themselves, and after a brief and no doubt inebriating period in which there was every appearance that their opinions might be taken seriously, they were told to be forevermore silent and their risen expectations were quashed. Yet far from resenting their jobs in the bureaucracy, they sought them out eagerly, regarding them as favors bestowed for special merit. And the general silence that ensued after 1792 was not the silence of despair or even, as is sometimes suggested,[18] the calm before the storm. Apart from the fairly obvious fact that a calm lasting more than half a century has an identity quite apart from the storm that may follow it, there was nothing sullen, resentful, or rebellious about the *Aufklärer* under Francis II. In part that was because their enthusiasm was quite effectively deflected by the war against France, patriotism being a well-known cure for discontent, and in part, no doubt, because they had good reason to feel that they had made their point: that whatever the momentary political mood, the essentials of the Josephinian system remained, a solid enough accomplishment for which, rightly or wrongly, they deemed themselves in part responsible. It was perhaps not the most admirable of attitudes, but men have behaved worse in easier circumstances.

18. Wangermann, *Joseph II to the Jacobin Trials,* p. 191.

Epilogue

ON FEBRUARY 20, 1790, Joseph II died. Four days later the semi-official *Wiener Zeitung* carried an obituary which, while praising the deceased, was careful to confine its praise to the most recent of his many reforms.[1] This, as all its readers were well aware, had been the rescript which annulled the greater part of his program in Hungary. Not many voices were raised in disagreement. One of the harshest balance-sheets was drawn up by Joseph's chief collaborator, Prince Kaunitz. In a note intended for the new ruler, Leopold II, but possibly never shown to him, Kaunitz accused Joseph of having been inflexible, excessively severe, hasty in his decisions, unwilling to consult expert opinion, and constantly in the grip of a veritable mania for change. Moreover, once he had made up his mind on a question no power in the world could get him to change it. The worst of it was that he was apt to make it up not only without consulting anyone, but without thinking the matter through himself.[2] Although the unmistakable odor of sour grapes clings to these lines, and there can be no question that Kaunitz had all along resented the tighter rein he had been under since the death of Maria

---

1. F. Engel-Janosi, "Josephs II. Tod in Urteil der Zeitgenossen," *M.I.Ö.G.*, XLIV (1930), 337.

2. Quoted in K. O. v. Aretin, *Heiliges Römisches Reich: 1776–1806* (2 vols., Wiesbaden, 1967), I, 204.

Theresa, he was only expressing, on the basis of intimate and firsthand knowledge, what amounted to the almost universal judgment of Joseph's contemporaries. Most of the biographies of the late Emperor that were now rushed into print, while steering clear of such implications of *lèse-majesté* as were included in the Chancellor's remarks, put Joseph down as a misguided enthusiast whose failures were the direct and inevitable results of his own shortcomings.[3]

It seemed as if Joseph had been abandoned by all but the unmistakable radicals, such as the ex-Franciscan Eulogius Schneider, who was later to be guillotined as a Jacobin in the Thermidorean reaction. Schneider, almost alone, bewailed the Emperor's passing. Joseph's voice had been almost alone in the German lands in defending the interest of common humanity:

> Wer hat so wie du gelitten,
> Wer für Weisheit so getritten,
> Wer das Gute so erstürmt.
>
> Hat nicht gegen deine Schlüsse
> Jezt die Bosheit Hindernisse
> Jetzt die Dummheit angethürmt.[4]

It would be sad if these rather awkward lines by a German radical, who was known in more conservative circles as "Die dichtende Hyäne" and who, so far as is known, had no close contacts whatever with Austria, would have to serve as the Emperor's epitaph.

Fortunately, in spite of their discouragement, and in spite of the political pressures prevailing, even in the brief reign of Leopold II, to dismiss Joseph with no more than routine praise, not all of the paladins turned their backs on their one-time hero. First among them Pezzl produced a reasonably fair-minded

3. Among others, J. F. Gaum, *Biographie Kaiser Josephs II. bis zu seinem Tode* (Frankfurt a. M. and Leipzig, 1790), Gaum's revenge for Joseph's stubborn neglect of his talents; and L. Hübner, *Biographie Kaiser Josephs II.* (Salzburg, 1790). At that, Hübner was the publisher of a Salzburg newspaper which was banned in Munich because of its liberal opinions.

4. E. Schneider, *Elegie an den sterbenden Kaiser Joseph II.* (Bonn, 1790).

evaluation of the Emperor's work.[5] Joseph, he maintained, had been faithful all his life to the Cameralist maxim of *Österreich über alles, wenn es nur will.* He had always intended to lift his people up into the light. His failures had been mainly the result of faulty tactics, his reliance on all too imperfect assistants to carry out his work. Also, Austria's neighbors, worried about the possible effects of her resurgent powers, concentrated their energies on the frustration of Joseph's intentions. The unremitting increase in prices that had contributed so much to his unpopularity should be blamed on them rather than on him. It was not strictly true, either, that Joseph had been oblivious of the opinion in which he was held by the educated world. His secretaries had standing orders to point out for his perusal all articles commenting on his policies in such journals as the *Teutscher Merkur,* the *Staatsanzeigen,* and the *Ephemeriden.* It was, to be sure, disappointing that he had insisted on disregarding the opinions of journalists and pamphleteers in his own dominions, that he had not realized that they were in the position of molding public opinion either favorably or unfavorably to his program. He had been too impatient, too zealous, too determined to economize, not on behalf of himself, it was true, but for the good of his people. But all these were forgivable sins.

A little later Huber published a very similar analysis.[6] It was a major paradox, he wrote, that a prince who had done so much for his people should have died unmourned by so many of them. Joseph's main failing had been an unwillingness to recognize that he had set himself an impossible task. Thus, he had been all too ready to criticize deficiencies in his servants, whose failures had in fact been inevitable. It was small wonder that he had come almost to hate a people which had resisted with all its might his efforts to make it happy.

Both of these analyses were, if sympathetic, relatively unsophisticated. To blame Joseph's troubles on the suspicion of

5. J. Pezzl, *Charakteristik Josephs II.* (Vienna, 1790).
6. F. X. Huber, *Geschichte Josephs II.* (Vienna, 1792).

his fellow monarchs and on the conservatism of the majority of his subjects might be not entirely an inaccuracy, but was not describing anything beyond the obvious and immutable. Anyone else would have labored under the same handicaps, anyone else would have failed just as completely. It was again Joseph Richter who produced a more detailed and perceptive summation and epitaph, and it is only right that he should have the last word.[7]

On the far side of the river Styx, ladies of quality and common burghers, artisans and scholars, Capuchins and Jews, walk arm in arm. They are waiting for the last judge, Minos, to decide their fates. It soon emerges that their amiability is not to be traced to the fact that the grave abolishes all differences of status and class, but is merely a belated attempt to convince their judge of the genuine depth of their Christian sentiments. Richter, who is allowed to wander through this landscape, notices among those souls already condemned to hell several of his acquaintances from among the Viennese clergy. Their punishment consists of being obliged to read through all of the *Wiener Kirchenzeitung* each day for all of eternity. At this point there is a stir; an important personage, Joseph himself, has arrived. Richter trembles for his fate: had he not, in the course of his life, angered countless people who will undoubtedly now avail themselves of the opportunity to testify against him? He consoles himself with the reflection that kings, like nature, frequently are forced to do people harm so that good may emerge. Perhaps this will be taken into consideration.

The first witness against the Emperor is not long in appearing; he is, as might have been guessed, a priest. He rattles off a litany of Joseph's transgressions against the church. By far the worst of his sins, he maintains, had been the abolition of the censorship. This had exposed his subjects to the full impact of the seductive voice of reason. Just as God had already punished

7. J. Richter, *Kaiser Joseph der Zweite vor Minos Richterstuhl* (Frankfurt a. M. and Leipzig, 1791).

this impious ruler during his life by saddling him with countless afflictions, he should be damned for all eternity.

The second accuser is an aristocrat. He objects that throughout the course of history princes have always regarded the nobility as the chief pillars of their thrones and rewarded them
accordingly. So long as this wise system had been in effect, the
state had run smoothly, the monarch had been undisturbed in
the exercise of his powers, the bourgeoisie had stayed within its
proper bounds, held in check by respect and obedience, and the
peasants had remained in the conditions Heaven had intended
for them, stupidity and slavery. Joseph insisted on pulling down
this time-honored structure because of the unjustified fear that
the aristocracy was preparing itself to challenge the royal power.
In order to humble it he had done away with serfdom, and in
so doing, had compromised the whole system: the peasant had
hardly had time to become aware that he was once more being
considered as a human being before he started demanding that
the common rights of humanity be extended to him too. The
next and fatal step had been for the peasant to lose his awe of
the landlord, who in his eyes now became merely another man.

The third accuser, a long-time servant of Maria Theresa's,
whom Joseph at his accession had summarily deprived of his
pension, tells of having been reduced to penury and of finally
having been unable to prevent his daughters from going on the
street to bring money into the house.

The fourth is a merchant, who laments that his profits were
more than cut in half by Joseph's decree forbidding the impor-
tation of foreign goods. He had not been able to acquire the
country estate which would have been his with only one more
year of high profits. He reports that to his certain knowledge the
edict had not even benefited his manufacturing friends, because
Joseph had given in to the unhappy notion of making it possible
for little men to borrow enough money to start manufactures of
their own, the effect having been to drive prices down.

There are others who complain that the Emperor arbitrarily increased already stiff sentences imposed on them by the courts; that they had been unjustly dismissed from their positions; that, without having been guilty of the least transgression, they had been replaced in their jobs by deserving military men.

At last, Joseph is asked what he has to say in reply: "Nothing" is his answer; it is quite clear that his defense is implicit in the accusations themselves. But Richter is unwilling to let it go at that. Joseph's guardian angel now descends from heaven to plead for him. True, he says, the Emperor dissolved many monasteries, but this must be put in the balance against the many new churches which he built and the dramatic expansion in the numbers of the parish clergy for which he was responsible. In allowing the press to be free, he had merely restored a right of which his subjects had been unjustly deprived by his predecessors. So far as religious toleration went, princes have no right to be more godly than God, who is evidently content to be worshiped in a variety of ways. Furthermore, Joseph had by no means been an enemy of the nobility, but rather had been its admirer in all instances where its services merited admiration. The abolition of serfdom had done no more than put an end to a notorious misuse of nobiliar power. The curtailment of pensions had, admittedly, been harsh and had resulted in the commission of many injustices, but it had resulted also in the reduction of a seriously inflated budget. And the prohibition of imports had been objected to only by those who consistently put their selfish interests before those of the nation.

Thereupon, Minos decides that Joseph is fully worthy of spending eternity in the Elysian fields, where he is triumphantly conducted by all present.

It is no more than fitting that this vindication of Joseph should have come at the hands of a man who, as we have seen, had abandoned almost all hope for the success of his program while he still lived; who had reached the conclusion that the tasks which the Emperor had set himself were not realistically to be accomplished; and who now, since it was the fashion to mock the Josephinian reforms as gross exaggerations going counter to the Austrian grain, pointed out that if Joseph had erred, it had been only out of an excess of humanity and compassion. Perhaps Richter's judgment was not strictly accurate. But it was psychologically acute, bittersweet, and very Austrian.

Bibliography

A. CONTEMPORARY PUBLICATIONS

Alxinger, J. B. v. *Doolin von Mainz.* Leipzig, 1786.

———. *Bliomberis.* Leipzig, 1791.

———. *Anti-Hoffmann.* 2 vols. Vienna, 1792.

Ayrenhoff, C. v. *Sämmtliche Werke.* 4 vols. Vienna and Leipzig, 1789.

Blumauer, A. *Sämtliche Werke.* 9 vols. Munich, 1827.

Born, I. v. *Travels through the Bannat of Temesvar, Transylvania and Hungary in the Year 1770.* Trans. R. E. Raspe. London, 1777.

Breitkopf, J. G. I. "Ueber Buchdruckerey und Buchhandel in Leipzig." *Journal für Fabrik, Manufaktur und Handlung,* V (1793).

Brettschneider, H. G. v. *Die Religion mit philosophischen Augen betrachtet.* Vienna, 1774.

———. *Fabeln, Romanzen und Sinngedichte.* Frankfurt a. M. and Leipzig, 1781.

Eybel, J. V. (Zakkaria). *Briefe aus Rom über die Aufklärung in Oesterreich.* Frankfurt a. M. and Leipzig, 1785.

Fessler, I. A. *Was ist der Kaiser?* Vienna, 1782.

———. *Marc-Aurel.* 4 vols. 2nd ed. Breslau, 1793.

Friedel, J. *Briefe über die Galanterien von Berlin.* Gotha, 1782.

———. *Briefe aus Wien verschiedenen Inhalts an einen Freund in Berlin.* Pressburg, 1783.

———. *Christel und Gretchen: Eine ländliche Posse.* Vienna, 1785.

Gaum, J. F. *Gespräch im Reiche der Toten zwischen Maria Theresia und Friedrich dem Zweyten.* 5 vols. Malta [Ulm], 1786–87.

———. *Biographie Kaiser Josephs II. bis zu seinem Tode.* Frankfurt a. M. and Leipzig, 1790.

Gedanken über einige dem Publikum sehr nützliche Verbesserungen in Wien. Vienna, 1783.

Geiger, C. I. *Reise eines Erdbewohners in den Mars.* Facsimile ed. J. Hermand. Stuttgart, 1967.

Die Gimpelinsel, oder der Stiefbruder des Linnäus. Vienna, 1782.

Gute Nacht, oder Vertheidigung der äusserst verletzten Ehre der bürgerlichen Schneider in Wien. Vienna, 1781.

Huber, F. X. *Herr Schlendrian, oder der Richter nach den neuen Gesetzen.* 2nd ed. Berlin, 1787.

———. *Geschichte Josephs II.* Vienna, 1792.

Hübner, L. *Biographie Kaiser Josephs II.* Salzburg, 1790.

Kratter, F. *Briefe über den itzigen Zustand von Galizien.* 2 vols. Leipzig, 1786.

———. *Das Schleifermädchen aus Schwaben.* 2 vols. Frankfurt a. M., 1790.

Mayern. W. F. v. *Dya-Na-Sore.* 5 vols. Frankfurt a. M., 1787.

Pezzl, J. *Marokanische Briefe.* 2nd ed. Frankfurt a. M., 1784.

———. *Faustin oder das philosophische Jahrhundert.* 3rd ed. Vienna, 1785.

———. *Charakteristik Josephs II.* Vienna, 1790.

———. *Beschreibung und Grundriss der Haupt- und Residenzstadt Wien.* 3rd ed. Vienna, 1809.

Rautenstrauch, J. *Das neue Wien, eine Fabel.* Vienna, 1785.

———. *Die Verbannung der Jesuiten aus China.* Constantinople, 1785 [Vienna, 1786].

———. *Wie lange noch?* Vienna, 1786.

Richter, J. *Der Gläubiger.* Vienna, 1773.

———. *Reise von Wien nach Paris.* Vienna, 1781.

———. *A. B. C. Buch für grosse Kinder.* 2 vols. Vienna, 1782.

Richter, J. (Obermayer). *Bildergalerie katholischer Misbräuche.* Vienna, 1784.

Richter, J. *Der gewöhnliche Wiener mit Leib und Seele.* Vienna, 1784.

Richter, J. (Schmidt, F.). *Vertheidigung der Wiener und Wienerinen.* Vienna, 1784.

Richter, J. *Warum wird Kaiser Joseph von seinem Volke nicht geliebt?* Vienna, 1786.

———. *Herr Kaspar.* Vienna, 1787.

———. *Kaiserin Maria Theresia's Wiederkehr nach der Oberwelt.* Vienna, 1788.

———. *Kaiser Joseph der Zweite vor Minos Richterstuhl.* Frankfurt a. M. and Leipzig, 1791.

———. *Die Eipeldauer Briefe: 1785–1797.* Ed. E. v. Paunel. 2 vols. Munich, 1917–18.

Schneider, E. *Elegie an den sterbenden Kaiser Joseph II.* Bonn, 1790.

Sonnenfels, J. v. *Grundsätze der Polizey, Handlung und Finanzwirtschaft.* 3 vols. 3rd ed. Vienna, 1770.

———. *Über die Abschaffung der Folter.* Vienna, 1775.

———. *Ueber die Ankunft Pius VI. in Wien.* Vienna, 1782.

———. *Gesammelte Schriften.* 10 vols. Vienna, 1783–87.

Trenck, F. v. der. *Meine Gedanken über die unsichtbare Leibeigenschaft des Königreichs Böhmen.* Vienna, 1782.

Ueber das Recht des Landesfürsten in Betreff der dogmatischen Bullen. Vienna, 1781.

Der 42. jährige Affe. Ein ganz vermaleidetes Märchen. Berlin [Prague], 1784.

Vorschlag eines patriotischen Oesterreichers für Joseph II. Vienna, 1782.

Watteroth, H. J. *Für die Toleranz überhaupt und Bürgerrecht der Protestanten in katholischen Staaten.* Vienna, 1781.

Weidmann, P. *Johann Faust.* Prague, 1775; ed. R. Payer v. Thurn, Vienna, 1911; ed. K. Adel, Vienna, 1964.

———. *Der Misbrauch der Gewalt.* Vienna, 1778.

Wieland, C. M. *Der goldene Spiegel.* Leipzig, 1772.

Wucherer, G. P. *Beweis, das Zahlheim als ein Opfer der Unwissenheit seiner*

Richter und durch Gewalt des Stärkeren hingerichtet wurde. Ostahiti [Vienna], 1786.

B. SECONDARY LITERATURE

1. Articles

Barton, P. F. "Ignatius Aurelius Fessler." *Kirche im Osten,* VII (1964).

Bauer, R. "Les Épopées de Johann Baptist von Alxinger." *Études Germaniques,* VI (1951).

———. "Le Joséphisme." *Critique,* XI (1958).

Benda, K. "Probleme des Josephinismus und des Jakobinerthums in der Habsburgischen Monarchie." *Südost-Forschungen,* XXV (1966).

Bernard, P. P. "Heresy in Fourteenth Century Austria." *Medievalia et Humanistica,* X (1956).

———. "Jerome of Prague, Austria and the Hussites." *Church History,* XXVII/1 (1958).

———. "The Origins of Josephinism: Two Studies." *Colorado College Studies,* VII (1964).

———. "Joseph II and the Jews: The Making of the Toleration Patent of 1782." *Austrian History Yearbook,* IV/V (1970).

Bruggemann, F. "Der Kampf um die bürgerliche Welt- und Lebensanschaung in der deutschen Literatur des 18. Jahrhunderts." *D.V.L.G.,* III/1 (1925).

Daly, J. J. "The Poet of a Lost Camelot." *Thought,* XIII (1938).

Demelius, H. "Beiträge zur Haushaltsgeschichte der Universität Wien." *Studien zur Geschichte der Universität Wien,* I (1965).

Deutsch, G. "Joseph v. Sonnenfels und seine Schüler." *Ö.U.R.,* n.F., V (1888).

Dörrer, F. "Römische Stimmen zum Frühjosephinismus." *M.I.Ö.G.,* LXIII (1955).

Engel-Janosi, F. "Josephs II. Tod im Urteil der Zeitgenossen." *M.I.Ö.G.,* XLIV (1930).

Fournier, A. "Gerhard van Swieten als Censor." *Sitzungsberichte der Kaiserlichen Akademie der Wissenschaften, Philosophisch-historische Classe,* LXXXIV (1876).

Grünberg, K. "Franz Anton von Blanc: Ein Sozialpolitiker der Theresianischen-Josephinischen Zeit." *Jahrbuch für Gesetzgebung, Verwaltung und Volkswirtschaft im deutschen Reich,* n.F., XXXV (1911).

Gugitz, G. "Die Wiener Stubenmädchenliteratur von 1781." *Zeitschrift für Bücherfreunde,* VI/1 (1902).

———. "Johann Friedel." *J.G.G.,* XV (1905).

———. "Johann Pezzl." *J.G.G.,* XVI (1906).

———. "Lorenz Leopold Haschka." *J.G.G.,* XVII (1907).

———. "Alois Blumauer." *J.G.G.,* XVIII (1908).

———. "Franz Kratter." *J.G.G.,* XXIV (1913).

Hoffmann, A. "Österreichs Wirtschaft im Zeitalter der Aufklärung." *Ö.G.L.,* XII/5 (1968).

Langsam, W. C. "Emperor Francis II and the Austrian 'Jacobins,' 1792–1796." *American Historical Review,* L (1945).

Lederer, M. "Die Gestalt des Naturkindes im 18. Jahrhundert." *Programm der K. K. Staats-Oberrealschule in Bielitz,* XXXII (1908).

Lefèbvre, G. "Le Despotisme éclairé." *Annales Historiques de la Révolution Française,* XXI (1949).

Lhotsky, A. "Ein Bericht über die Universität Göttingen für den Staatskanzler Fürst Kaunitz-Rietberg 1772." *Festschrift Percy Ernst Schramm.* 2 vols. Wiesbaden, 1964.

Maass, F. "Vorbereitung und Anfänge des Josephinismus." *M.Ö.S.,* I/2 (1948).

―――. "Die österreichische Jesuiten zwischen Josephinismus und Liberalismus." *Zeitschrift für katholische Theologie,* LXXX (1958).

Menhofer, E. "Österreich im Reiseführer Thomas Nugents." *Bausteine zur Geschichte Österreichs.* Vienna, 1966.

Meyer, F. H. "Zur Geschichte der österreichischen Bücherpolizei." *Archiv für Geschichte des deutschen Buchhandels,* XIV (1891).

Mühlher, R. "Die Literatur zur Zeit der Aufklärung in Österreich." *Ö.G.L.,* VIII/6 (1964).

Müller, P. "Der aufgeklärte Absolutismus in Österreich." *Bulletin of the International Committee of Historical Sciences,* IX/1 (1937).

Payer v. Thurn, R. "Paul Weidmann, der Wiener Faust-Dichter des 18. Jahrhunderts." *J.G.G.,* XIII (1903).

―――. "Eine politische Denkschrift Paul Weidmann's." *J.G.G.,* XVI (1906).

Pongratz, W. "Geschichte der Universitätsbibliothek." *Studien zur Geschichte der Universität Wien,* I (1965).

Probst, E. "Johann Baptist von Alxinger." *J.G.G.,* VII (1897).

Raumer, K. v. "Absoluter Staat, Korporative Libertät, Persönliche Freiheit." *H.Z.,* CLXXXIII/1 (1957).

Rommel, O. "Der Wiener Musenalmanach." *Euphorion,* Ergänzungsheft VI (1906).

―――. "Rationalistische Dämonie: Die Geister-Romane des ausgehenden 18. Jahrhunderts." *D.V.L.G.,* XVII (1939).

Schenk, H. G. "Austria." In A. Goodwin, ed. *The European Nobility in the Eighteenth Century.* London, 1953.

Schmidt, L. "Blumauer und das Volkslied." *Germanisch-romanische Monatsschrift,* XXVIII (1940).

Silagi, D. "Ungarn und der geheime Mitarbeiterkreis Kaiser Leopolds II." *Südosteuropäische Arbeiten,* LVII (1961).

Strasser, K. "Die 'Predigerkritiken': Ein Beitrag zur Geschichte des Josephinismus." *Jahrbuch des Vereines für Geschichte der Stadt Wien,* XI (1954).

Sturmberger, H. "Studien zur Geschichte der Aufklärung des 18. Jahrhunderts in Kremsmünster." *M.I.Ö.G.,* LIII (1939).

Voltelini, H. v. "Die naturrechtlichen Lehren und die Reformen des 18. Jahrhunderts." *H.Z.,* CV (1910).

Wagner, H. "Der Höhepunkt des französischen Kultureinflusses in Österreich in der zweiten Hälfte des 18. Jahrhunderts." *Ö.G.L.,* V/10 (1961).

―――. "Der Einfluss von Gallikanismus und Jansenismus auf die Kirche und den Staat der Aufklärung in Österreich." *Ö.G.L.,* XI/10 (1967).

Walter, F. "Die zensurierten Klassiker." *J.G.G.,* XXIX (1930).

Wiedemann, Th. "Die kirchliche Bücher-Censur in der Erzdiöcese Wien." *A.Ö.G.,* L (1873).

Wilhelm, G. "Briefe des Dichters Johann Baptist von Alxinger." *Sitzungsberichte der philosophisch-historischen Classe der kaiserlichen Akademie der Wissenschaften, Wien,* CXL (1899).

Wodka, J. "Die Kirche und die Aufklärung." *Ö.G.L.,* X/5 (1966).

Wytrzens, G. "Sur la sémantique de l'Aufklärung." In P. Francastel, ed. *Utopie et institutions au xviiie siècle*. Paris and The Hague, 1963.

Zenker, E. V. "Geschichte des Wiener Zeitungswesens von seinem Anfängen bis zum Jahre 1800." *Ö.U.R.*, n.f., X (1891).

Zöllner, E. "Bemerkungen zum Problem der Beziehungen zwischen Aufklärung und Josefinismus." *Österreich und Europa*. Graz, Vienna, and Cologne, 1965.

2. Books

Abafi, L. *Geschichte der Freimaurerei in Oesterreich-Ungarn*. 5 vols. Budapest, 1890–97.

Aretin, K. O. v. *Heiliges Römisches Reich: 1776–1806*. 2 vols. Wiesbaden, 1967.

Arneth, A. v. *Geschichte Maria Theresias*. 10 vols. Vienna, 1863–79.

———. *Maria Theresia und Joseph II.: Ihre Correspondenz*. 3 vols. Vienna, 1867–68.

Bartels, A. *Freimaurerei und deutsche Literatur*. Munich, 1929.

Becker, E. D. *Der deutsche Roman um 1780*. Stuttgart, 1964.

Benedikt, E. *Kaiser Joseph II.: 1741–1790*. Vienna, 1936.

Benedikt, H. *Franz Anton von Sporck*. Vienna, 1923.

Bernard, P. P. *Joseph II and Bavaria*. The Hague, 1965.

———. *Joseph II*. New York, 1968.

Bibl, V. *Kaiser Joseph II.: Ein Vorkämpfer der Grossdeutschen Idee*. Vienna and Leipzig, 1943.

Boos, H. *Geschichte der Freimaurerei*. 2nd ed. Aarau, 1906.

Brunner, S. *Die Mysterien der Aufklärung in Österreich: 1770–1800*. Mainz, 1869.

Bulling, K. *Johann Baptist von Alxinger*. Leipzig, 1914.

Droz, J. *L'Allemagne et la Révolution Française*. Paris, 1949.

Eder, K. *Der Liberalismus in Altösterreich*. Munich and Vienna, 1955.

Ellemunter, A. *Antonio Eugenio Visconti und die Anfänge des Josephinismus*. Graz and Cologne, 1963.

Emmerich, K. *Der Wolf und das Pferd: Deutsche Tierfabeln des 18. Jahrhunderts*. Berlin, 1960.

Engel, L. *Geschichte des Illuminaten-Ordens*. Berlin, 1906.

Epstein, K. *The Genesis of German Conservatism*. Princeton, 1966.

Faÿ, B. *La Franc-Maçonnerie et la révolution intellectuelle du 18e siècle*. 2nd ed. Paris, 1961.

Féjtö, F. *Un Hapsbourg révolutionnaire: Joseph II*. Paris, 1953.

Fischer-Colbrie, A. *Michael Denis: Im schweigendem Tale des Mondes*. Graz and Vienna, 1958.

Flygt, S. G. *The Notorious Dr. Bahrdt*. Nashville, Tenn., 1963.

Frank, G. *Das Toleranz-Patent Kaiser Josephs II*. Vienna, 1882.

Frank, H. J. *Catherina Regina von Greiffenberg*. Göttingen, 1967.

Gagliardo, J. G. *Enlightened Despotism*. New York, 1967.

Gnau, H. *Die Zensur unter Joseph II*. Strasbourg and Leipzig, 1911.

Goldfriedrich, J. *Geschichte des deutschen Buchhandels: 1740–1804*. Leipzig, 1909.

Gooch, G. P. *Germany and the French Revolution*. London, 1920.

Görlich, E. J. *Einführung in die Geschichte der österreichischen Literatur*. Vienna, 1946.

Gräffer, F. *Josephinische Curiosa*. 5 vols. Vienna, 1848–50.

Gugitz, G. *Das Wertherfieber in Oesterreich*. Vienna, 1908.

Guglia, E. *Maria Theresia.* 2 vols. Munich and Berlin, 1917.

Gulyga, A. W. *Der deutsche Materialismus am Ausgang des 18. Jahrhunderts.* Trans. I. Bauer and G. Korf. Berlin, 1966.

Gutkas, K. *Geschichte des Landes Nieder-Oesterreich.* 3 vols. Vienna, 1959.

Hamberger, G. C. *Das gelehrte Teutschland.* 24 vols. Lemgo, 1796–1834.

Hanfstaengl, E. F. S. *Amerika und Europa von Marlborough bis Mirabeau.* Munich, 1930.

Hennings, F. *Und sitzet zur linken Hand: Franz Stephan von Lothringen.* Vienna, Berlin, and Stuttgart, 1961.

Hermand, J. *Von Deutscher Republik: 1775–1795.* 2 vols. Frankfurt a. M., 1968.

Hofmann-Wellenhof, P. v. *Michael Denis.* Innsbruck, 1881.

Holzknecht, G. *Ursprung und Herkunft der Reformideen Kaiser Josefs II. auf kirchlichem Gebiete.* Innsbruck, 1914.

Im Hof, U. *Isaak Iselin und die Spätaufklärung.* Berne and Munich, 1967.

Kann, R. A. *A Study in Austrian Intellectual History.* New York, 1960.

Keil, R. *Wiener Freunde, 1784–1808.* Vienna, 1883.

————. *Aus klassischer Zeit: Wieland und Reinhold.* 2nd ed. Leipzig, 1890.

Kerner, R. J. *Bohemia in the Eighteenth Century.* New York, 1932.

Kimpel, D. *Der Roman der Aufklärung.* Stuttgart, 1967.

Kink, R. *Geschichte der kaiserlichen Universität zu Wien.* 2 vols. in 3. Vienna, 1854.

Krauss, W. *Die französische Aufklärung im Spiegel der deutschen Literatur des 18. Jahrhunderts.* Berlin, 1963.

Krieger, L. *The Politics of Discretion.* Chicago and London, 1965.

Krones, F. v. *Geschichte der Karl-Franzens Universität in Graz.* Graz, 1886.

Kuess, G., and B. Scheichelbauer. *200 Jahre Freimaurerei in Österreich.* Vienna, 1959.

Kürschner, J. *Deutsche National-Literatur.* 163 vols. Berlin, 1884–93.

Lennhoff, E. *Die Freimaurer.* 2nd ed. Zurich, Leipzig, and Vienna, 1929.

Lhotsky, A. *Österreichische Historiographie.* Vienna, 1962.

Lux, J. A. *Ein Jahrtausend österreichischer Dichtung.* 2nd ed. Vienna, 1948.

Maass, F. *Der Josephinismus: Ursprung und Wesen.* 5 vols. Vienna, 1951–61.

————. *Der Frühjosephinismus.* Vienna and Munich, 1969.

Macartney, C. A. *The Habsburg Empire: 1790–1918.* London, 1968.

Magris, C. *Der Habsburgische Mythos in der österreichischen Literatur.* Trans. M. v. Pasztory. Salzburg, 1966.

Mentschl, J., and G. Otruba. *Österreichische Industrielle und Bankiers.* Vienna, 1965.

Mikoletzky, H. L. *Österreich, das grosse 18. Jahrhundert.* Vienna, 1967.

Mitrofanov, P. v. *Joseph II.: Seine politische und kulturelle Tätigkeit.* Trans. V. v. Demelic. 2 vols. Vienna and Leipzig, 1910.

Müller, W. *Josef von Sonnenfels.* Vienna, 1882.

————. *Gerhard van Swieten.* Vienna, 1883.

Nadler, J. *Buchhandel, Literatur und Nation in Geschichte und Gegenwart.* Berlin, 1932.

————. *Literaturgeschichte Österreichs.* 2nd ed. Salzburg, 1951.

Nagl, J. W., J. Zeidler, and E. Castle. *Deutsch-Österreichische Literaturgeschichte.* 4 vols. Vienna and Leipzig, n.d.

Nussbaumer, E. *Geistiges Kärnten.* Klagenfurt, 1956.

O'Brien, C. H. *Ideas of Religious Toleration at the Time of Joseph II: A Study of the Enlightenment among Catholics in Austria. Transactions of the American Philosophical Society*, N.S., LIX/7 (1969).

Osterloh, K. H. *Joseph von Sonnenfels und die österreichische Reformbewegung im Zeitalter des aufgeklarten Absolutismus.* Lübeck and Hamburg, 1970.

Padover, S. K. *The Revolutionary Emperor: Joseph II of Austria.* 2nd ed. New York, 1967.

Pastor, L. v. *The History of the Popes from the Close of the Middle Ages.* Trans. E. F. Peeler. 40 vols. London, 1891–1953.

Pfister, K. *Maria Theresia: Mensch, Staat und Kultur der spätbarocken Welt.* Munich, 1949.

Pichler, C. *Denkwürdigkeiten aus meinem Leben.* Ed. E. K. Blümml. 2 vols. Munich, 1914.

Pirchegger, H., J. Mayer, and F. Kaindl. *Geschichte und Kulturleben Österreichs.* 3 vols. 5th ed. Vienna and Stuttgart, 1960.

Rieder, H. *Wiener Vormärz.* Vienna, 1959.

Rieser, H. *Der Geist des Josephinismus.* Vienna, 1963.

Rommel, O. *Die Alt-Wiener Volkskomödie.* Vienna, 1952.

Sashegyi, O. *Zensur und Geistesfreiheit unter Joseph II.* Budapest, 1958.

Sauer, E. *Die französische Revolution von 1789 in zeitgenössischen deutschen Flugschriften und Dichtungen.* Weimar, 1913.

Scheel, H. *Süddeutsche Jakobiner.* Berlin, 1962.

Schneider, F. J. *Die Freimaurerei und ihr Einfluss auf die geistige Kultur in Deutschland am Ende des 18. Jahrhunderts.* Prague, 1909.

Schottenloher, K. *Flugblatt und Zeitung.* Berlin, 1922.

Schreyvogl, F. *Ein Jahrhundert zu früh: Das Schicksal Josephs II.* Vienna, Berlin, and Stuttgart, 1964.

Schwarz, J. *Geschichte der Savoy'schen Ritter-Akademie in Wien.* Vienna and Leipzig, 1897.

Sengle, F. *Wieland.* Stuttgart, 1949.

Silagi, D. *Jakobiner in der Habsburger-Monarchie.* Vienna and Munich, 1962.

Small, A. W. *The Cameralists.* Chicago and London, 1909.

Spiel, H. *Fanny von Arnstein oder die Emanzipation.* Frankfurt a. M., 1962.

Stiehler, G. *Beiträge zur Geschichte des vormarxistischen Materialismus.* Berlin, 1961.

Strakosch, H. E. *State Absolutism and the Rule of Law.* Sydney, 1967.

Tomek, E. *Kirchengeschichte Österreichs.* 3 vols. Innsbruck, Vienna, and Munich, 1935–59.

Valjavec, F. *Der Josefinismus.* 2nd ed. Munich, 1945.

———. *Die Entstehung der politischen Strömungen in Deutschland: 1770–1815.* Munich, 1951.

Voegt, H. *Die deutsche Jakobinische Literatur und Publizistik.* Berlin, 1955.

Walter, F. *Wien.* 3 vols. Vienna, 1940–44.

———. *Die Theresianische Staatsreform von 1749.* Vienna, 1958.

Wandruszka, A. *Österreich und Italien.* Vienna, 1958.

Wangermann, E. *From Joseph II to the Jacobin Trials.* 2nd ed. Oxford, 1969.

Wenck, W. *Deutschland vor hundert Jahren.* 2 vols. Leipzig, 1887, 1890.

Werner, R. M. *Aus dem Josephinischem Wien.* Berlin, 1888.

Wiese, B. v. *Politische Dichtung Deutschlands.* Berlin, 1931.

Winter, E. *Joseph II.: Von den geistigen Quellen und letzten Beweggründen seiner Reformideen*. Vienna, 1946.

———. *Der Josefinismus*. 2nd ed. Berlin, 1962.

———. *Frühaufklärung*. Berlin, 1966.

———. *Frühliberalismus in der Donaumonarchie*. Berlin, 1968.

Wodka, J. *Kirche in Österreich*. Vienna, 1959.

Wolff, H. M. *Die Weltanschaung der deutschen Aufklärung in geistlicher Entwicklung*. 2nd ed. Berne and Munich, 1963.

Wolfsgruber, C. *Christian Anton Kardinal Migazzi*. Ravensburg, 1897.

Wurzbach, C. v. *Biographisches Lexicon des Kaiserthums Oesterreich*. 60 vols. Vienna, 1856–91.

Zellwerker, E. *Das Urbild des Sarastro: Ignaz von Born*. Vienna, 1953.

Zenker, E. V. *Geschichte der Wiener Journalistik von den Anfängen bis zum Jahre 1848*. Vienna and Leipzig, 1892.

Zimburg, H. v. *Die Geschichte Gasteins und des Gasteiner Tales*. Vienna, 1948.

Zitzenbacher, W. *Joseph Richter, bekannt als Eipeldauer*. Graz and Vienna, 1957.

Index